Machine Quilting
Solutions

ECHNIQUES FOR FAST & SIMPLE TO AWARD-WINNING DESIGNS

Christine Maraccini

C&T PUBLISHING

Text © 2007 Christine Maraccini

Artwork © 2007 C&T Publishing, Inc.

Publisher: Amy Marson

Editorial Director: Gailen Runge

Acquisitions Editor: Jan Grigsby

Editor: Kesel Wilson

Technical Editors: Carolyn Aune and Ellen Pahl

Copyeditor/Proofreader: Wordfirm Inc.

Cover Designer: Kristen Yenche

Design Director/Book Designer: Kristen Yenche

Illustrator: Kirstie L. Pettersen

Production Coordinator: Kirstie L. Pettersen

Photography: Luke Mulks & Diane Pedersen, unless otherwise noted

Published by C&T Publishing, Inc., P.O. Box 1456, Lafayette, CA 94549

Front cover: *May Baskets*, © 2006 Christine Maraccini

Library of Congress Cataloging-in-Publication Data

Maraccini, Christine.
  Machine quilting solutions : techniques for fast & simple to award-winning designs / Christine Maraccini.
    p. cm.
  ISBN-13: 978-1-57120-392-2 (paper trade : alk. paper)
  ISBN-10: 1-57120-392-3 (paper trade : alk. paper)
  1. Machine quilting. 2. Machine quilting--Patterns. I. Title.

  TT835.M27225 2007
  746.46--dc22

2006026065

Printed in China
10 9 8 7 6 5 4 3

Contents

Dedication

This book is dedicated to my husband, Tony. Words are not adequate enough to thank you for all that you do. Not only are you my best friend, but you are the foundation from which I am able to fly. You constantly push me to live to my potential, and for that I'll always be grateful.

Also to the three most extraordinary people I know: Bruno, Gianna, and Angelo. It is my greatest honor and privilege to be your mom. You inspire me to imagine, dream, and reach. Everything I do is for you.

Acknowledgments

I'd like to express a very special thank-you to the marvelous people who pieced quilts for this book:

Bruce Bennett, the master of enthusiasm and guru of the yo-yo quilt—I feel privileged to know a person with such a big heart and artistic talent.

My darling Diane Woods—your friendship is a treasure, and I'm honored that you have blessed me with it. I knew you would do a great job and you surpassed my expectations.

Linda Morris—you have encouraged and cheered me on since the beginning. I could never thank you enough for your tireless hard work. You are a jewel.

The masterful Christie Batterman—you agreed to tackle the most difficult quilt and made it look easy. Your expertise and magic touch made my job so much easier.

My dear friend Cheryl Uribe—not only did you help make and bind quilts for this book, but you were there for me every moment I needed a pep talk or a friend to bounce an idea off. You keep me laughing and are my reliable confidant. Thanks for taking this journey with me; it just wouldn't have been the same without you.

Many thanks and kudos go to Elizabeth Cofer. You did a fabulous job on all those bindings.

I'd like to recognize Laura Lee Fritz and Ron Paul for their contributions to this art form. You have opened the door for quilters like me to create new and innovative techniques.

I would also like to express my appreciation to Alex Anderson, whose wisdom and advice came at the very moment I needed it most.

Special acknowledgment goes to Bob and Heather Purcell at Superior Threads for their technical advice and expertise. A greater understanding of thread and how it works makes us all better quilters.

And, of course, thanks go to everyone at C&T who placed their faith in me—especially Kesel Wilson, who swooped in to pull this project together at the twelfth hour.

Introduction

How many quilt tops do you have tucked away waiting to be quilted? I always have a few that are awaiting that final blessing. *You know, it's really not a quilt until it's quilted!* Because of that I like to call these unfinished masterpieces "tops" instead of quilts. I've found that an overwhelming majority of "quilters" are actually "toppers." They lack the know-how to get it done themselves, so some send their tops to professionals to be quilted. Others put away their tops unfinished. That's where I come in. I believe that everyone, with a little instruction, is capable of quilting his or her own tops.

Have you ever walked through a quilt show and wondered how those other people came up with the designs for their quilting? It's really much easier than you'd think. Most of us turn to books and formal patterns to figure out what to quilt. Finding the designs isn't really the hard part. *Learning how to choose a design for your particular quilt is the real challenge.* This book will introduce you to a method for "decoding" your quilt tops and choosing the right quilting designs for your special creations.

You need to begin looking at your quilts in a new way. Discover the paths and basic shapes that make up your quilt. See how the designs affect the overall picture. Consider the fabrics and the threads. Take into account how the quilt will be put to use. Together we are going to break the quilting process down so that you can learn to look at any quilt and figure out how to quilt it.

Once you have learned to pick appropriate designs, it's time to actually quilt them. You can handle it—I promise. It's just that most of us tend to put the cart before the horse. 'Fess up! How many of you have walked over to your machine and actually attempted to quilt a flower with no prior knowledge of how to draw that flower? You have no plan—you think you are just going to walk over and start quilting something cool. Ha! Don't worry; I'm guilty too. I'm going to teach you how to learn these designs so that you can actually quilt them freehand on your own. I know the tricks and I can't wait to share them with you!

I have taught countless students to machine quilt and I know you can learn this skill too. My favorite moment is when a student successfully quilts a flower for the first time. I want you to experience that for yourself. I know that you can do this. Let's get started!

The Basics of Machine Quilting

Throughout my quilting career I have quilted on both a domestic (tabletop) and a longarm machine. I'd like to take a moment to debunk the myth that a longarm machine is a magical tool that produces amazing quilting. A longarm quilting machine does make machine quilting more convenient and efficient. However, it is not necessary to use a longarm machine to achieve beautiful quilting. Everything in this book can be done on either a domestic or a longarm machine. The quality of the quilting is dependent on you and your ability to freehand draw the designs that you choose to quilt, not on the technology of the machine that you are using.

TIPS FOR FREE-MOTION QUILTING ON A DOMESTIC MACHINE

Quilting Feet

For free-motion quilting you will need a free-motion or darning foot for your machine. My favorite ones have a clear ring or oval that presses against the fabric as you sew. These are great because they enable you to see where you are going. Usually the circle on the bottom of the foot has a relatively accurate measurement of $1/4$ inch in radius, which can come in handy as a spacer when you are echo quilting. Each brand of sewing machine has specific feet that will fit on it. See your local sewing machine dealer to get the correct foot for your personal machine.

Each brand of machine has its own quilting feet. I prefer the type with a clear ring or oval.

Your Working Style & Your Work Space

One of the biggest complaints about machine quilting is the difficulty of maneuvering a large quilt under the short arm of a domestic sewing machine. You will notice throughout this book that my working style is to quilt in continuous paths whenever possible. This enables me to roll the quilt so that just the path I need is exposed. I can start at one end of the quilt and sew one design, non-stop, until I reach the other end of the quilt. I hate to start and stop, so I try to do it as little as possible. Remember, our goal is to get these quilts finished!

Your workstation can be either fancy or simple as long as it has a flat surface behind and to the left of your sewing machine large enough to hold the weight of your *entire* quilt as you sew. I quilt at my kitchen table with my sewing machine located at the front right corner of the table.

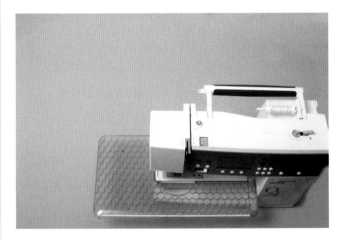

Your workstation can be simple or fancy. I prefer simple, so a large table and a machine with a nice extended base are perfect.

When I have an especially large quilt I add another table to the back of my kitchen table to increase the surface area. I also like to use an extended base on my sewing machine when I'm quilting. This extra surface allows me to maintain better control over the area I'm quilting.

If your quilt seems to be sticking to the extended base, wipe the base with a small amount of Pledge cleaner and the surface will become slicker. As you would after contact with any chemical, be sure to wash your quilt when completed to remove any residue.

Guiding Your Quilt

When free-motion quilting, you will need to make a frame using your hands. This allows you to maintain control over the space that you are quilting and holds the three quilt layers in place as you sew. Always maintain a good frame with constant pressure as you quilt. Do not grab the quilt and pull it as you work; this will only distort the quilting and shift the layers out of alignment. You will need something to put on your hands to help grip the fabric as you sew. Most common are quilting gloves or rubber fingertips. I also like to put lotion on my hands or use the pink finger moistener found in business supply stores. Please use these with caution and wash your quilt after it is finished to remove any oily residue.

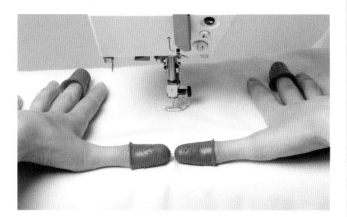

Build a good frame with your hands while quilting. Tugging and pulling can distort your quilt.

TIPS FOR FREE-MOTION QUILTING ON A LONGARM MACHINE

The most commonly used longarm machines in the industry have the following things in common: a large throat, long canvas leaders to pin your quilt layers to, and a smooth carriage system to move the machine while you sew. I prefer to "float" my quilt tops on my longarm machine. This means that I pin the backing fabric onto the leaders. I then lay the layer of batting onto the backing near the top leader and then lay the quilt top onto the batting. I pin the quilt top through the batting and onto the backing. I allow the quilt top to drape over the front edge of the machine. This allows me to adjust the quilt top as I work. I can fix any spots that are uneven or have extra fullness as I move down the quilt.

The most important thing I can tell you about using a longarm is that it takes practice. These are not magic machines. The general rule is that it takes one full year to become comfortable and proficient on a longarm. You will get better each time you finish a quilt. Ask your local quilt guild if they have charity quilt tops that need to be quilted. This is a great opportunity to get in some extra practice. Also, take lessons from experienced teachers who are familiar with the brand of machine you use. Be sure to take a maintenance class for your machine as well. Take time to learn how your machine operates in the specific climate and conditions that it is in. Because a longarm has so many moving parts and tension dials, you need to practice and experience how *your* machine works in order to truly get the most from this wonderful piece of equipment.

STARTING & STOPPING

How to start and stop, that is the question! I'm not happy if my starts and stops are visible. In fact, most quilt show judges are not happy to see these either. Whether on a longarm or a domestic machine, I use a method that involves what I've been told is a hand-quilting knot. Always start quilting in a spot that's easy to hide, such as a seam or the base of a leaf or flower. When starting, I drop the needle and raise it so that I can pull the bobbin thread to the top of the quilt.

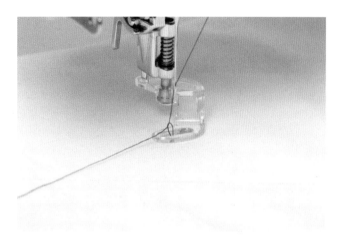

Pull the bobbin thread to the top.

I hang onto the two tails (bobbin and needle threads), then drop the needle back into the exact same hole that I pulled the bobbin thread through earlier. Hang on tight to the tails so that you don't get a nest of thread on the back of your quilt! Start sewing from that point. Once you have laid down a few inches of stitching, it's safe to let go of the tails and tie them off. Tie a square knot (left over right, then right over left), landing the knot exactly over the hole that your stitching started at. Pop the threads through a self-threading needle.

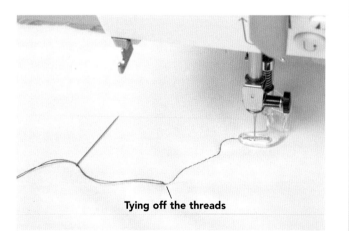

Tying off the threads

Slide that needle under the top layer of your quilt, starting at the hole where you began sewing, and proceed in the direction of your quilting.

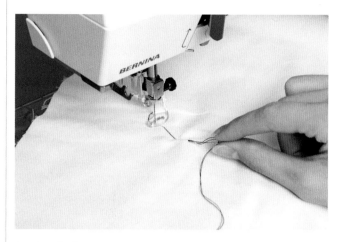

Burying the knot

Pull the needle out an inch or two away from where you began. Give the needle a little tug and the square knot will pop into the hole where you began sewing. Clip these threads close to the top of the quilt and the thread will disappear. When you run out of thread in your bobbin or spool, or stop quilting, use the same process. If you don't have long enough tails of thread, unsew back to a good junction (the base of a leaf, a seamline, etc.) then pull the bobbin thread to the top and continue from there.

Thread & Fabric

Don't forget the thread! This is the final artistic element that you get to add to your masterpiece.

Traditional quilting has often neglected the artistic element that thread can add to a quilt. It seems like many quilters thought that beige was the only color of thread on the market. Worse yet, many quilters used that clear stuff so that they could hide their quilting. Although these threads have their place, I say it's time to revolt! There are many new types of thread on the market, and it's time we show off our quilting and use some of them. Break out the bright variegated threads or test that metallic thread you've been intimidated by. You work hard to make your topstitching designs pretty, so make sure they can be seen.

THE ROLE OF THREAD, NEEDLES, AND FABRIC

If you own a sewing machine it is important to know and understand the basic principles of thread and needles, and their relationship with fabric.

Friction & Thread Breakage

The top thread goes through the needle and fabric several times before it finally gets to stay there. The friction of the fabric scraping the thread can break it. Even if it doesn't break, it can be shredded, which means that your quilting is weak and might not stand the test of time. For this reason use a large needle with a deep groove. The large needle will punch a larger hole in the fabric, reducing the amount of friction from the thread passing through the hole. The deep groove also protects the thread by sheltering it from the rough edges of the hole. My needle of choice for general quilting is an 80/12 topstitch sharp or metallic needle. Don't worry about the large holes left in the fabric; these will close up with washing or they can be steamed closed.

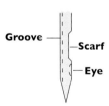

Close-up of the tip of a needle

Another thing to consider is the type of thread you are using and whether you are sewing on a domestic or longarm machine. Different threads have varying strengths and thicknesses, which must be considered when choosing the appropriate needle. To make your decision easier, I've included a handy reference chart to guide you in the needle selection process.

General needle guidelines for various threads

THREAD TYPE	DOMESTIC MACHINE NEEDLE	LONGARM MACHINE NEEDLE	REASON
Standard-size cotton and matte polyester (looks like cotton)	Topstitch 80/12 sharp	Sharp 18 (MR 4.0)	Requires a medium- to large-diameter needle
Shiny polyester (looks like silk) and dissolvable	Topstitch 90/14 sharp or metallic	Sharp 16 (MR 3.5)	Requires a smaller-diameter needle
Extra-thick cotton and metallic	Topstitch 90/14 sharp or metallic	Sharp 19 (MR 4.5)	Requires a larger needle

Tension

When you change the thickness of the thread, the top tension needs to be adjusted to compensate. If you have been piecing with a standard thread and change to a thick thread, the tension discs need to be loosened to accommodate the thicker thread. Not only will the thicker thread cause a tension increase, but the tension discs will also flatten the thread. Flattened thread has a tendency to shred since it doesn't move through the needle properly.

> When your tension is off, the rule of thumb is this:
>
> Too much top thread showing on the back of the quilt
>
> = tighten your top thread (higher tension number).
>
> Too much bobbin thread showing on the top of the
>
> quilt = loosen your top thread (lower tension number).
>
> On a domestic machine, a low tension number equals
>
> looser tension. A high tension number equals
>
> tighter tension.

Luckily, you will seldom need to change the tension on the bobbin thread on a domestic machine. Try adjusting the top tension first. If the bobbin thread is stronger than the top thread, it will cause your top thread to break; however, it's perfectly okay if the bobbin thread is not as strong as the top thread. Unless you're sewing with metallic thread, it's usually okay to use the same thread in the bobbin as you are using in the top. When using metallic in the top, use silk-style polyester in the bobbin.

Many factors affect the tension in a longarm machine. The general rules for thread and tension mentioned above apply to a longarm as well as a domestic machine. Refer to the reference guides for your particular brand and model for the finer details. Always test the tension prior to quilting, even if you haven't changed threads. Factors such as temperature and humidity can affect the thread and the many moving parts of your machine. My favorite trick is to take all that leftover batting I have lying around and cut it into small squares the size of my hand. I have a basket of these next to my machine and I use them to test my thread tension and clean any oil residue from the needle prior to quilting.

UNRAVELING THE MYSTERY OF FANCY THREAD

The Value of Quality

The most important thing to keep in mind when considering fancy thread is to get the good stuff. *It's worth your time and money to purchase quality thread.* You will encounter less breakage and your finished product will be more durable. It has taken a tremendous amount of time and energy to make your quilt; it would be foolish to save a couple of dollars on an inferior thread for the quilting. Second-rate threads have a greater tendency to break and shred while you quilt with them. The time you save with less breakage will surely pay the cost of higher-quality thread.

My favorite brand of thread is Superior Threads. Almost every bit of stitching in this book was done with this brand of thread. Although there are other quality threads on the market, I prefer Superior Threads because I've experienced the quality of these threads and I know that they will perform as they should.

Cotton Threads

Cotton threads come in solid and variegated colors as well as a variety of thicknesses. A good-quality cotton thread is made of long- or extra-long-staple cotton. The staple is the length of the cotton fiber used to make the thread. The longer the staple, the fewer the lengths of fiber twisted together. This means greater strength and less lint. When using 100% cotton threads I prefer extra-long-staple Egyptian cotton or high-quality long-staple cotton. If the label on the end of the spool doesn't give you the staple length, you can assume that it is short-staple cotton and is an inferior thread. Never use glazed cotton for machine quilting; it can gum up your tension discs, the needle, and the bobbin works of your machine.

Synthetic Threads

My other favorite threads are made of polyester or a blend of polyester and cotton. I avoid rayon threads, which have a reputation for being weak, becoming brittle over time, not being heat resistant, and not being colorfast. Polyester threads can be made with a matte finish to look and act like cotton threads and produce little or no lint. Polyester threads also come in a shiny finish to look like silk. Because of its strength, polyester can be made in many different thicknesses to fit different uses. The thinnest polyester threads are terrific for trapunto work.

Metallic Threads

Metallic thread is intimidating to many quilters. When used sparingly, metallic thread can add that extra oomph that your quilt needs. When choosing a metallic thread, look for a thread with a nylon core and an outer protective surface. Test metallic thread for suppleness. It should drape and move like a standard thread does. If you pull some off the spool and it maintains its coil, put it back on the shelf and move on. I use Superior brand metallic threads with a lot of success.

I use a 90/14 metallic needle for metallic threads. This type of needle has an extra-deep groove to protect the thread. Drop the top tension all the way down to 1 or 2 on a standard sewing machine and begin test sewing. Slowly bring the tension up until you find what works best for your machine. Write down the tension so that you won't have to go through this process again. When using metallic thread in the top, fill your bobbin with a good-quality silk-style polyester thread.

I like to write the tension setting directly on the spool end so that I know where to find it next time.

Fiction: 100% cotton thread is the only thread that is safe to use on a cotton quilt. Synthetic thread can "cut" the fibers of your quilt fabric.

Fact: It's perfectly okay to use modern threads made of synthetic materials. In order to prevent the thread from cutting the fabric, the fabric and thread need to be similar in strength. The good-quality threads on the market have been manufactured and tested to be safe in your quilts.

FABRIC

The first step toward fantastic machine quilting is to start with good-quality fabric. Some fabrics are more abrasive than others. Many of the inexpensive bargain fabrics on the market are the biggest problem. I'm sure there is a good explanation for why this is so; I've just had too many bad experiences with these types of fabrics to waste my energy on them. The money you save will not be worth it when you try to quilt and your thread keeps breaking. Do yourself a favor, and piece your quilts with good-quality, supple fabrics. When you are ready to quilt them, you will be able to focus on the designs instead of spending your time trying to figure out why your thread is breaking again and again.

Another type of fabric that can be difficult to quilt on is batik. Oh, batiks are beautiful, but be prepared to treat them with special care. Because batik has such a tight weave, your needle will actually puncture the batik instead of sliding between the weave. This makes a very jagged hole for the thread to pass through, and therefore is quite abrasive on the thread. Think "sandpaper."

If you encounter either of these fabric issues and have thread breakage, you will need to slow down. When quilting on batik you should free-motion quilt at about half the speed you are used to. You can also spray a mixture of one part fabric softener to two parts water onto the fabric. Let it dry completely prior to quilting. This seems to lubricate the fabric so the thread can pass through without so much friction. If you are working on a longarm machine, your quilt should hang looser than normal and not be stretched taut on the leaders. This will help prevent the needle from bending, which can cause a disastrous needle break.

The Method to My Madness

WHAT IS YOUR QUILT'S DESTINY?

One of the most important aspects of quilting is choosing designs that are appropriate for the particular quilt you are working on. It's the quilt's purpose in life that ultimately dictates the style and density of the quilting it needs, so it is important to consider how the quilt will be used. I use three definitions to help me decide how much or how little quilting a top needs:

The Dragger

This is a quilt that is going to be dragged around and loved. Maybe it's going off to college to spruce up a dorm room. Whoever will be using it will likely wash it and toss it in the dryer. It will certainly be seeing a lot of use. This type of top usually needs some kind of edge-to-edge quilting pattern. Medium-density quilting is best so that the quilt has air pockets to hold warmth. Besides, nobody wants to cuddle up in a quilt that has been quilted so densely it feels like cardboard.

The Keepsake

This quilt is special, but you don't want to spend *too* much time on it. This is the type of quilt you would make as a gift for someone special or something you may occasionally hang in your house. It may even land on a bed or sofa and may get a moderate amount of use. For this type of quilt I like to add borders or large-scale quilting that fits the shapes in the quilt. I generally like to use medium-density quilting to help the quilt remain warm and cuddly. This type of quilt is a good opportunity for you to try out some fancier quilting designs without having to spend months quilting fine details.

The Showstopper

This quilt is going to be entered in a show and you want to win! This is a prized heirloom and the quilting will be its crowning glory. The cat will never get to take a nap on this one! For these types of quilts, the quilting is very dense and the designs should be intricate, theme appropriate, and original. It's also time to start thinking about including some trapunto. This is the technique of quilting beautiful motifs in a raised or extra-stuffed fashion. Don't give me that deer-in-the-headlights look. Trapunto is fun and easy as long as you follow the easy machine-quilting tricks found in this book (see page 84).

THE KEY TO DECODING

Once you know the quilt's destiny you need to "decode" the top. What this means is that most quilts have common shapes. By figuring out which shapes your top has, you can begin to choose appropriate designs to quilt into those shapes. Always have a plan. It's heartbreaking to start quilting a top and then realize later it could have been easier and quicker if it had been done another way. We want our quilts finished.

With a small amount of planning we can make machine quilting quicker, easier, and more fun!

tip

Choosing an appropriate quilting pattern for your quilt top begins with laying out the top and analyzing it. This is probably not how you have done it in the past. Most quilters commonly decide they want a floral motif or a geometric motif or some other motif before they analyze their quilt. Try to shift your process. Lay out the quilt. Instead of admiring your lovely piecing or focusing on the designs in the gorgeous fabric you used, look at the basic shapes. I mean really look. Are there squares? Be sure to notice the big ones *and* the little ones.

Keep your eye out for circles, triangles, and squares-on-point. Notice the paths. Some are wide, some are thin, and some are very obvious, such as sashings and borders. Some are hidden, such as the path left by piecing Sawtooth Stars side by side. Don't go too big here; we are looking for the shapes we can fit reasonably sized quilting designs into.

One quilt can have many options for paths and shapes. Choose the ones you think will emphasize the feeling you intended to communicate when you pieced the top. Be careful to choose the shapes and paths that will allow you to quilt as densely or sparsely as your quilt needs. Always remember that long paths are good when you are trying to get a quilt done quickly. They enable you to roll your quilt and get it ready to go under the arm of your machine, then to sew a large area without stopping to readjust the quilt.

This Log Cabin quilt is in the Barn Raising layout. This layout leaves us with a large square in the center. Of course it could also be treated as four triangles. There are large paths created by the colored fabrics and medium-width paths created by the light fabrics. Both of these could be extended into the border instead of treating the border as its own path. Each of the four corners has a small triangle.

Basic Log Cabin layout

The Block-on-Point layout (with Basket blocks) has obvious large squares set on point. Even the Basket block is in a square. The setting triangles are open triangle shapes but can

also be treated as partial squares. The baskets themselves are made up of many triangles and paths, and you can use these areas to quilt in small details.

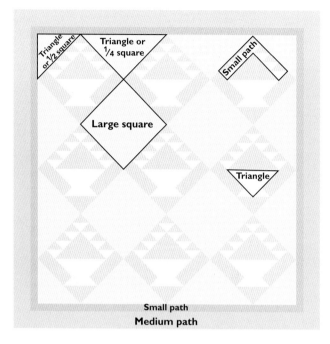

Basic Block-on-Point layout

This Irish Chain layout makes some interesting shapes. Notice that there are four complete squares-on-point and eight partial squares. Those areas could also be treated as twelve complete circles. Notice that the chain blocks can form a medium to large path or be broken into separate square units.

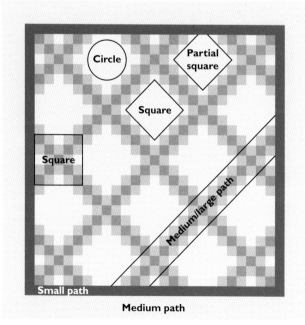

Basic Double Irish Chain layout

The Sawtooth Star layout contains a strange "path" or chain. Notice the square-on-point path running between the stars. Also consider that there are medium paths running diagonally in both directions across the quilt. If these paths were quilted, the squares-on-point would remain. This could make for an interesting quilt.

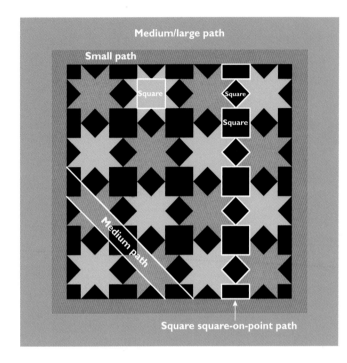

Basic Sawtooth Star layout

The Pinwheel layout contains a couple of irregular shapes. The eight-pointed pinwheel can be treated as a pinwheel or as a circle. The odd background shape can be treated as the odd shape it is, or it can be a square. This quilt could also be quilted in alternating large and medium-width paths either vertically or horizontally. If going this route, try alternating threads to enhance the effect.

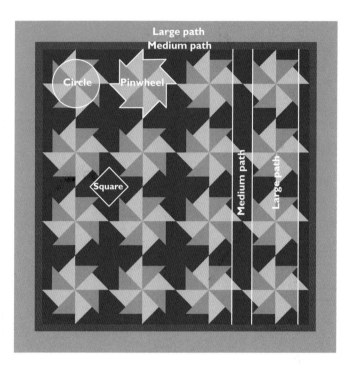

Basic Pinwheel layout

The Butterfly or appliqué layout has clearly defined squares and paths. Keep in mind that appliqué usually requires detail quilting, so you will likely not be treating the Butterfly blocks as the squares that they are. Additionally, you have the option of either quilting a special element in the corner-stones or including them in the paths that the sashing forms.

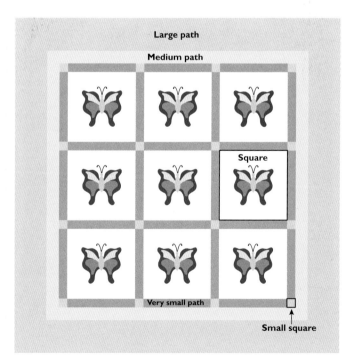

Example of an Appliqué layout

Auditioning a Design & Making Your Map

Take out a blank sheet of paper and draw an informal sketch of your quilt. Another quick trick is to photocopy a picture of the quilt if you're using a design from a magazine or book. No need to be fancy here; this is going to be your personal map for the quilt. Draw simple sketches of your quilting plans onto the map or on Quilter's Vinyl (see Resources, page 94) Audition quilting that is designed to fit into the shapes in *your* quilt. This way you can see which quilting design works best with the existing geometry and color of the quilt's piecing pattern. Also critical: you can see firsthand if your design will work *before* the sewing begins, allowing you to make changes freely.

In this book you will find all sorts of quilting options for the basic shapes found in your quilts. Although I have used specific patterns to illustrate the quilting (i.e., Log Cabin, Irish Chain), the quilting designs are interchangeable and can be used on any quilt. As you become familiar with my decoding technique you will begin to find quilting designs in books and magazines and better understand how to apply them to your own quilts.

At this point you can focus on designs that have a theme to match the fabric and mood of your particular quilt (e.g., floral, geometric). You will begin to notice that some shapes need a feature element such as a bouquet of flowers or a feather and that some areas need to be filled in to help draw the focus to these feature elements.

Borders

A special note on borders: I like to freehand quilt almost everything; it's much quicker than marking the motifs onto the quilt. Freehand can get a little tricky, though, when you have repeated motifs in a border. Measure your border and subtract the space needed for your binding. Find a good common denominator that will give you enough space for the motifs you plan to quilt. For example, on the *Kensington Cottage* 3 quilt, I was able to have a scrollwork border motif placed every 2″ on the inner border. This worked great because the piecing was a 1″ grid, meaning that there were little 1″ squares lined up right next to the border. Without marking anything, I was able to center one curl of each scrollwork piece over the 1″ squares of the quilt. When the piecing doesn't give me clear spacing guides I will either place pins along the border to remind me where my boundary is or I will draw a dot with a water-soluble pen. Don't get too fussy with the marking; you just need a general idea of the spacing. This process will help your borders be evenly spaced and neat while not interfering with the quick and easy freehand-quilting process.

Scrollwork border from Kensington Cottage 3, page 47

CHOOSING APPROPRIATE THREAD

After auditioning the design you want to use, you need to choose the appropriate thread for your quilting. However, I have a warning for you: Now that you have run out and purchased all those cool threads, you need to know *when* to use them. Take a deep breath and listen; this is an important rule. *Variegated threads look great on solid-colored fabrics. Solid-colored threads look great on printed fabrics.* I know it's tempting to find a really cool variegated thread that has all the same colors as your variegated, blended quilt. Please don't waste your time. That thread will simply disappear on your quilt. Solid fabrics, or fabrics that *read* solid, are the perfect canvas for that really cool variegated thread. When piecing your quilt, add a few spots that have a relatively solid fabric so you can quilt something unique and showcase your threads and design. If you simply have to use that variegated thread that matches your variegated quilt, consider using a relatively solid-colored backing and put that variegated thread in the bobbin.

Variegated thread seems to disappear on variegated fabric, as shown in the top quilting line. If you want the quilting to be seen, it's best to choose a solid thread color, as shown at the bottom.

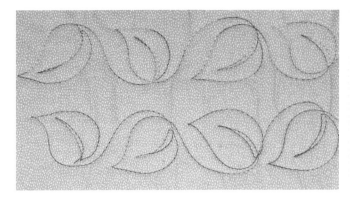

Variegated thread looks best on solid-colored fabrics.

DEVELOPING "MUSCLE MEMORY"

As you begin to practice and learn the designs in this book you will likely start to compare your artwork to mine. *Please* don't do that to yourself. You are a unique individual and your artwork should be as unique as you are. Think of it like this: your signature has your own personal flair and so does mine. Therefore your drawings (and quilting) should have your own personal flair, not mine. When I'm teaching you to draw a leaf, it's the general shape that you need to learn; the style should be all yours. Your goal should not be to exactly copy my leaf but to discover what *your* leaf looks like. Your quilting should be as distinct as you are instead of an attempt to create a carbon copy of someone else's work.

Christine Maraccini   Cheryl Uribe   Tony Maraccini

Notice each person's unique style.

Have you ever tried to free-motion quilt your signature? How about a morning glory? It's probably a lot easier to quilt your signature since you already know how to draw it. You likely don't have any idea how to draw a morning glory. So, it's a good assumption that if you teach your brain and the muscles in your hand to draw a particular design, it will be easier when it comes time to quilt that design. Therefore, it is a necessary step to learn the design prior to attempting to quilt it. *Don't skip this crucial step.* It is the single most important thing that you will do on your journey to learning to free-motion quilt.

First, make an enlarged photocopy of the motif you have chosen to practice. Then, take a clear piece of heavy plastic (page protectors work great) and place it over the design you are going to learn. Using a dry-erase pen, trace over the design so that you can begin to feel the flow of the shapes. Do this several times until you are comfortable that you have the feel of the design. You are now ready to move on to a blank canvas. Using a blank dry-erase board and dry-erase pen or a pen and paper, draw the design over and over and over on the blank canvas until you can do it without much thought. *This might take a while but it's worth your time.* It's sort of like learning to write your name in cursive for the first time. It probably took a while to learn but now you don't have to think about it at all.

If you plan to do a large edge-to-edge design, practice drawing the design on a large area so that you can feel the flow of how to continually change directions while maintaining an even density.

When doing edge-to-edge designs, I like to quilt in large 12″-wide paths across the quilt. I first move left to right in a large meandering motion, then return from right to left, zigzagging down the quilt until it's completed. It is good to practice this on paper first.

Practice on a dry-erase board many times before practicing with your sewing machine.

It's easier to quilt something that your brain has already been taught to draw.

Now you are ready to practice the design with your sewing machine. Load up sample fabric and batting on your longarm machine or make some practice pads (fabric-batting-fabric) to practice on your domestic machine. Your quilting will likely be a little uneven at first, but with practice it will smooth out. If you are quilting on a domestic machine keep in mind that a real quilt needs to be quilted in particular directions. Your little practice pad will fit neatly under the arm and does not mimic the feel of an actual quilt. For instance, if you are practicing a border design, don't move your practice pad left

and right. On a real quilt, you would need to move the quilt up or down to progress along the length of a border comfortably. Practicing under realistic conditions will better prepare you for executing the designs on a *real* quilt.

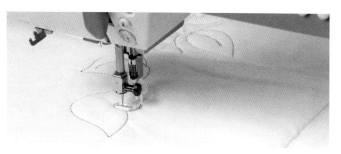

Once you feel comfortable drawing the design freehand, practice it on your sewing machine.

SNAPSHOT OF THE DECODING PROCESS

In summary, here are the steps to learning new motifs and becoming a confident quilter:

Step 1: Classify your quilt: Is it a dragger? A keepsake? A showstopper?

Step 2: Sketch a simple map of your quilt.

Step 3: Decode your quilt.

Step 4: Audition designs that will fit into the shapes of your decoded quilt top.

Step 5: Draw the designs onto the sketch of your quilt, creating a map.

Step 6: Choose appropriate thread styles and colors.

Step 7: Practice drawing your quilting designs on paper or a dry-erase board.

Step 8: Practice sewing the designs on practice pieces.

Step 9: Get to work quilting your prepared quilt top.

Look for these symbols next to the quilting motifs. They can help you choose the best motif for the shapes in your quilt.

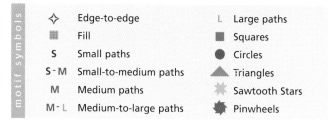

motif symbols				
◇	Edge-to-edge	L	Large paths
▦	Fill	■	Squares
S	Small paths	●	Circles
S - M	Small-to-medium paths	▲	Triangles
M	Medium paths	✳	Sawtooth Stars
M - L	Medium-to-large paths	✿	Pinwheels

Tahoe Retreat

TAHOE RETREAT 1, 2 & 3: 49″ x 49″

© 2006 Christine Maraccini

Pieced by Bruce Bennett, San Francisco, CA

Quilted by Christine Maraccini

Fabric by Timeless Treasures

TAHOE RETREAT 1: *Edge-to-edge free-motion quilting*

TAHOE RETREAT 1
"dragger"

The first quilt in this set is covered from edge to edge in a large Heat Wave pattern. This is a tried-and-true classic. Once you learn it, you are going to want to quilt everything with this motif. The Heat Wave pattern is a great option for masculine quilts and looks terrific on quilts with a lot of angles and straight seams, such as this traditional Log Cabin. Because it is such a busy quilting design, I like to make the thread blend in. It's not the thread that we are focusing on here; it's that lovely negative space that pops up between the lines of stitching.

Edge-to-Edge Heat Wave ✦ ▦

Heat Wave fill

1. Start by making a teardrop-shaped hook. Hook in the direction you are moving across the quilt. Once you complete the shape you will land pointing toward where you first hooked.

2. Now echo back over the hook. Try to keep the spaces between the echoes an equal width so your quilting looks consistent. A good rule of thumb is to use the foot of your machine as a guide to space the echoes.

3. Echo back over the hook again and you will have completed the motif and landed in the direction that you first hooked.

4. From this point, start the hook for the next motif.

5. Change directions often so you don't start forming a straight row of hooks. Although that makes a great border, our goal here is to fill the space.

As I quilt this motif I think: hook-one-two...hook-one-two... and so on. The hook-one-two is just a pattern, not a rule. When I quilt myself into a corner I echo an extra time to get myself out of the corner so I can start another motif.

TAHOE RETREAT 2
"keepsake"

TAHOE RETREAT 2: *Free-motion quilting of increasing intricacy*

Now that you have an idea of how to decode a quilt, it should be relatively easy to notice that there are very clear paths present. The second quilt in this set is relatively simple but utilizes those large light-colored paths to showcase a nice quilting design. Finally it's your chance to use that cool variegated thread that you've had stashed away for just the right quilt! Stitch those leaves in a gorgeous variegated thread and everyone will rave over your lovely designs. Fill the dark path with a matching thread in a dense version of the Heat Wave pattern that you learned for the first quilt. For the outer border, try the Heat Wave border, and your friends will be really impressed. It looks tricky, but after you practice it with pen and paper a few times you will catch on quickly.

Spike Leaf Border   M - L

This is a multipurpose medium- to large-path design. In this case I kept the leaves undulating when possible but pointed them into the corners when I reached the ends. Although this design is traditionally used as a border motif, here it works beautifully in the unconventional path found in a Log Cabin quilt. Please note that this is a directional design. When planning your quilting, be sure it is going in the direction you want and keep it consistent throughout the quilt.

Spike Leaf border

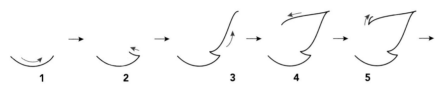

1. Start by sewing the bottom curve of the leaf.

2. Take a small bite in.

3. Curve back out and form a sharp point for the tip of the leaf.

4. Curve back down to form the other side of the leaf.

5. Sew out a little to form the barbed edge of the leaf.

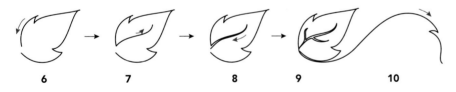

6. Now come back down and meet up with where you first started the leaf.

7. Give the leaf a nice curvy vein.

8. Backtrack along the vein. Don't worry about sewing exactly on your first stitch line. A little bit of fabric showing through helps the vein look natural.

9. Add 2 more curvy veins by sewing out and backtracking to the main vein and then back to the base of the leaf.

10. As you leave the leaf, be sure to curve the connector lines. That soft undulation will create a more graceful, organic look to your quilting. Continue to make the next leaf in the same way but with the leaf pointing down.

Heat Wave Border M-L

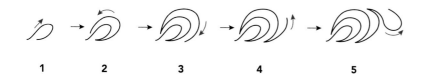

Heat Wave border

1. Create a teardrop-shaped hook.

2. Echo back once over the hook.

3. Echo back a second time over the hook.

4. Echo a third time, but only go halfway.

5. Create the next hook on the opposite side of the border.

6. Echo back once over this new hook.

7. Echo back a second time over the hook.

8. Echo a third time, but only go halfway.

9. Now make the third hook in the same direction as the first. Continue on in the same pattern.

TAHOE RETREAT 3
"showstopper"

TAHOE RETREAT 3: *Intricate free-motion quilting with trapunto*

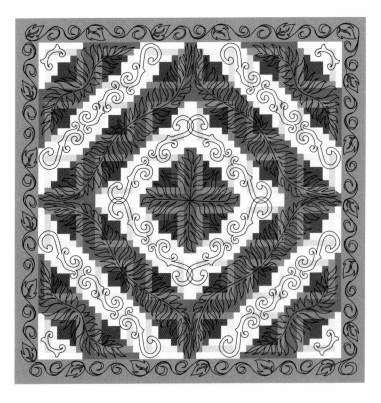

Usually I don't recommend trying trapunto on a quilt with so many seams, but this one just screams for it. Using a colored thread to outline the trapunto helps make it pop. Refer to page 88 for trapunto patterns A, B, and C for this quilt and to pages 84–87 for a step-by-step lesson on machine trapunto.

Modern Fern Feather   M - L

This modern variation of a feather resembles a fern and is a great option when working with fabrics with an autumn or forest theme. Practice it, and don't try to be perfect; it's *your* signature that we are looking for. Remember that nature isn't perfect; these designs look better when you let them flow and allow them to be organic.

Modern Fern Feather

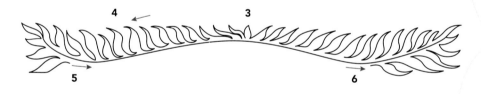

1. Begin at one end of the path and freehand sew a softly undulating center vein for the feather.

2. Once you reach the end of the vein, begin to sew long leaf shapes leaning away from the center of the feather, working your way back along the vein. Try not to touch the vein as you shape the spikes. An empty space along each side of the vein will make for a nicer-looking negative space.

3. Make note of where the center of the vein is. This is the one spot where the leaf shapes should point directly up and down.

4. After passing the vertical center leaf shape, begin to change the directions of the spikes, leaning them away from the center.

5. Once you reach the end of the vein where you began, be sure to stitch over the spot where you began to sew so you can hide your starting point. Sew around the end of the vein and start along the bottom of the vein.

6. Be sure to change the direction of the spikes at the center point and finish up as you reach the other end of the feather.

Spike Leaf Curl Border   M - L

These are those spike leaves again, mixed with two curls and sewn smaller. Try this with any leaf that you know how to sew. Add two curls like this one so that your leaves alternate directions, or add one curl so that all the leaves point the same way.

Spike Leaf Curl border

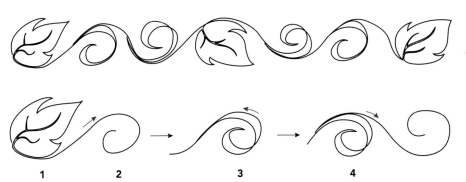

1   2   3   4

1. Follow the instructions for quilt #2 of this set (page 22) to form the leaves. Begin the border with a leaf.

2. Exit the leaf and change directions to form the first swirl.

3. Backtrack along the swirl. Don't try to trace exactly along the first stitched swirl; it is almost impossible. Besides, that graceful overlapping will make the swirl look more like a real tendril.

4. Exit the first swirl and change directions again to form the second swirl.

5   6

5. Trace back along this second swirl.

6. Exit the second swirl and change directions again to start the next leaf. If you changed directions with each shape, this leaf should be pointing in the opposite direction of the first leaf. Again, you will notice that this gentle undulation will give an organic flow to your quilting.

TAHOE RETREAT (BASIC LOG CABIN) PIECING

Quilt is 55″ × 55″

Blocks are 8″ × 8″

Outer border is 3½″ wide

Fabric

1½ yards total various off-white fabrics for logs

1¾ yards total various medium brown/green fabrics for logs

¾ yard dark brown fabric for center squares and binding

⅞ yard medium brown fabric for border

60″ × 60″ piece of batting

3⅓ yards backing fabric

Cutting

From the various off-white fabrics:

Cut 32 strips 1½″ × the width of the fabric. Subcut into the following pieces:

36 rectangles 1½″ × 2½″ (B unit)

36 rectangles 1½″ × 3½″ (C unit)

36 rectangles 1½″ × 4½″ (D unit)

36 rectangles 1½″ × 5½″ (E unit)

36 rectangles 1½″ × 6½″ (F unit)

36 rectangles 1½″ × 7½″ (G unit)

From the various medium brown/green fabrics:

Cut 38 strips 1½″ × the width of the fabric. Subcut into the following pieces:

36 rectangles 1½″ × 3½″ (C unit)

36 rectangles 1½″ × 4½″ (D unit)

36 rectangles 1½″ × 5½″ (E unit)

36 rectangles 1½″ × 6½″ (F unit)

36 rectangles 1½″ × 7½″ (G unit)

36 rectangles 1½″ × 8½″ (H unit)

From the dark brown fabric:

Cut 3 strips 2½″ × the width of the fabric. Subcut into 36 squares 2½″ × 2½″ (A unit).

From the medium brown border fabric:

Cut 6 strips 4″ × the width of the fabric.

Piecing

1. Start with the center square and piece each block in order according to the diagram, adding 1 log at a time around the block, turning a quarter-turn each time. Press the seam allowances away from the center square. Make 36 blocks.

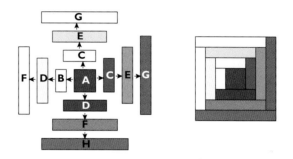

Piecing order for a Log Cabin block

2. Arrange the blocks according to the layout. Sew the blocks together in rows. Then sew the rows together to create the center of the quilt. Use conventional methods to attach the outer border.

Barn Raising layout for a Log Cabin quilt

May Baskets

MAY BASKETS 1, 2 & 3: 62˝ x 62˝
© 2006 Christine Maraccini

Pieced by Linda Morris, Orinda, CA

Quilted by Christine Maraccini

Fabric by RJR Fabrics

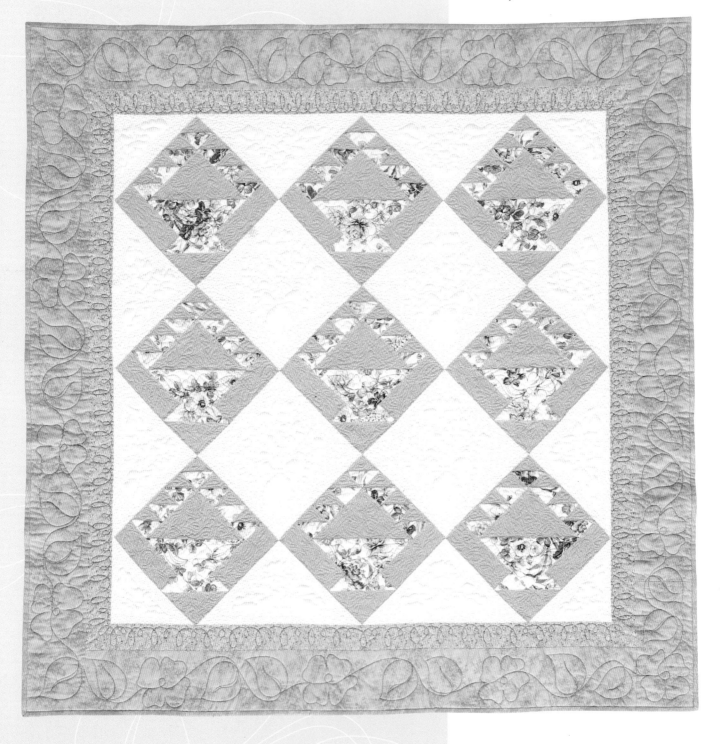

MAY BASKETS 1: *Edge-to-edge free-motion quilting*

MAY BASKETS 1
"dragger"

This design is the basic building block of the floral all-over designs. The pattern utilizes two main shapes and will produce a beautiful result. It can look sophisticated on this type of Block-on-Point quilt or be sweet and simple on a baby quilt. Watch your spacing and don't let this get really dense or it will take over.

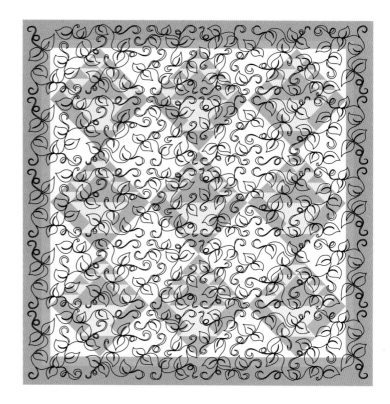

Edge-to-Edge Tendril Leaf ✧

Tendril Leaf fill

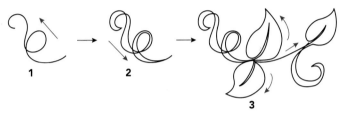

1. Swirl out, forming a loop, then change directions and create a curl.

2. Backtrack over the line you just made. Don't try to be exact; a little space between the lines gives the tendril some substance.

3. Now start your first basic leaf (see page 76 for a basic leaf). This is a simplified version of the one we learned earlier. After that leaf is done, start the next leaf in the opposite direction. This will create a cute double-leaf bundle. If you get stuck in a corner it's perfectly okay to do a single leaf to get yourself out.

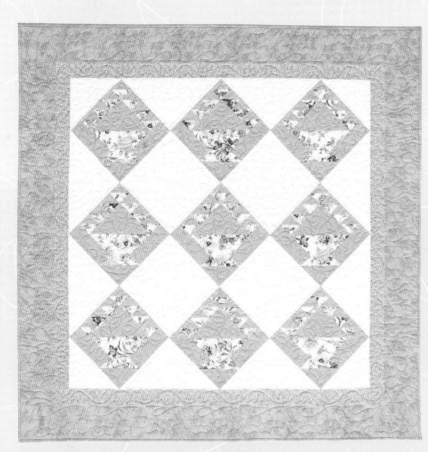

MAY BASKETS 2: *Free-motion quilting of increasing intricacy*

MAY BASKETS 2
"keepsake"

This quilt has large open squares set on point and some nice open borders to fill with beautiful florals. The Basket blocks can be treated like squares or as basket shapes. In this instance, I'm treating the baskets as baskets, quilting the leaves and tendrils as though they are coming out from the baskets. This motif is functional and pretty, but not too fussy. Use the same leaf quilting techniques you learned in the previous project to quilt these leaves coming out of the baskets.

Chrysanthemum in a Square ■ ● ▲

This is a cool trick to avoid having to start and stop. Make a small flower and continue adding petals until you fill the circle or square that it is being placed in. For the setting triangles, I quilted the shape as though it were just a portion of a square. Try this with different flower centers and petals to match the fabrics you used to piece the quilt.

Chrysanthemum in a Square

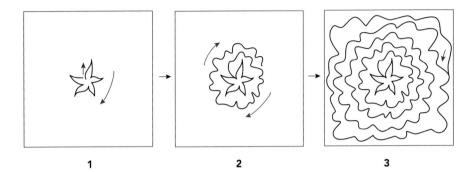

1   **2**   **3**

1. Start by creating a 5-pointed star in the center. Do this by creating small, skinny petal shapes radiating from the center. I think "head-arm-leg-leg-arm" then connect to my starting point. Be sure to leave empty space between the leaf shapes.

2. Once you have created the center, sew out and start making wavy petal shapes, radiating out and getting bigger as you go. Don't echo exactly over the first petals or the outer petals will be too big.

3. Fill the square with an even density of petals. Once the square is filled, end by attaching the last petal to one beneath it.

Baskets

Follow the instructions for quilt 1 of this set (page 30) to quilt the Basket blocks.

Example of a basket motif

Baskets

Crocus Border   M

This cute Crocus border is great for a medium-sized border or path. Use it on a tulip-themed quilt and the flowers will appear to be tulips.

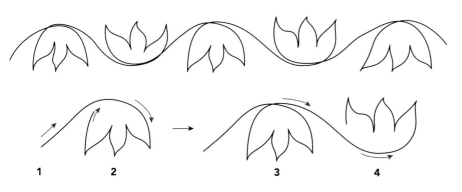

Crocus border

1. Start by making a large open curve in the direction you plan to move down the length of the border.

2. Create 3 petal shapes, bringing you back to the base of the crocus.

3. Cross over your original line, closing off the crocus.

4. Change directions and begin making the outermost petal of the next crocus. Continue on, changing directions with each flower.

Chrysanthemum Border   L

This design creates a nice texture on a quilt. As with any flower, change the shape of the petals and you will have a totally new design.

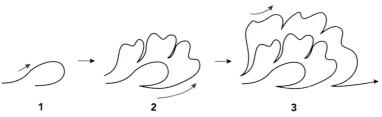

Chrysanthemum border

1. Create a hook facing the inside of the quilt.

2. Make 3 flower petals as you echo back toward the beginning of the hook. Don't touch the hook as you come in with the petals; you need the negative space to be left open.

3. Echo the petals back to the front of the hook. Now you are ready to make the next hook. Lovely!

MAY BASKETS 3
"showstopper"

MAY BASKETS 3: *Intricate free-motion quilting with trapunto*

I love quilts with blocks set on point. When I see the open space left between the blocks I know immediately that those squares need some trapunto. This quilt is so traditional that I like to stick with simple designs that maintain the sweet beauty of the fabric and piecing. This is a directional quilt; it has a definite top and bottom. A quick tip is to use a blue water-soluble pen to draw an arrow on the empty block indicating the direction. When your quilt is rolled up during the quilting, this will help you remember which direction your motif should go. Refer to pages 89–90 for the trapunto patterns A, B, and C for this quilt and to pages 84-87 for a step-by-step lesson on machine trapunto.

Rockrose Basket Detail

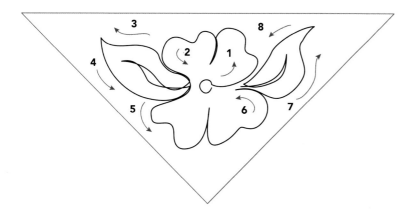

Rockrose basket detail

1. Create the center circle for the flower and head out to make the first petal.

2. Form the second petal and dip in a little short to leave room for the leaf.

3. Form a leaf pointing toward the top left corner of the triangle.

4. Make the other side of the leaf. When you reach the base, sew out and back to make a vein.

5. Create the third petal.

6. Create the fourth petal, dipping in early to leave space for the last leaf.

7. Form a leaf pointing toward the top right corner of the triangle.

8. Make the other side of the leaf. When you reach the base, sew out and back to make a vein.

Traditional e&l Border S

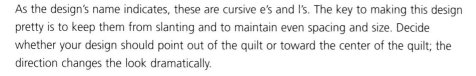

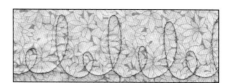

Traditional e&l border

As the design's name indicates, these are cursive e's and l's. The key to making this design pretty is to keep them from slanting and to maintain even spacing and size. Decide whether your design should point out of the quilt or toward the center of the quilt; the direction changes the look dramatically.

Rockrose Border M - L

This is my favorite border design for floral quilts. It's a flower-leaf-leaf combination. You can try any number of flower and leaf combinations to match your fabric and it will always look great.

Rockrose border

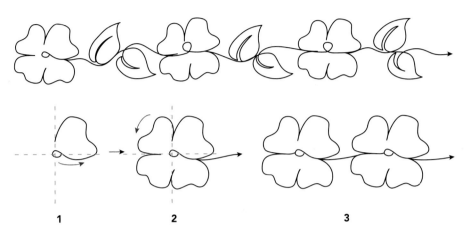

1. A rockrose is a 4-petal flower that is formed in quadrants. Imagine that there are axis lines on your quilt running parallel to and perpendicular to the border (blue dashed lines in the diagram). Start by creating a center circle for the first flower. Sew out along the axis in the direction you will proceed down the border. Form the first petal in the upper right quadrant, dipping in at the perpendicular axis line.

2. Continue on to create the next 3 petals, filling the quadrants and dipping in at the axis line. As you come in from making the last petal, touch the first petal and sew away from the flower to start the center of the next flower.

3. A row of these flowers would have a relatively straight line connecting them. Add 2 leaves (see page 30) that change directions between the flowers and you have a nice flower-leaf-leaf border.

Leaf Echo Micro-fill

This quilt needs tight quilting that will depress the area around the basket. I used a trapunto fill that I call Leaf Echo Micro-fill. Refer to pages 86–87 to learn this fill and the other trapunto fills that are handy for blocks like this Basket block.

MAY BASKETS
(BASIC BASKET-ON-POINT) PIECING

Quilt is 56½″ × 56½″

Blocks are 10″ × 10″

Inner border is 2″ wide

Outer border is 5″ wide

Fabric

¾ yard floral fabric for baskets

1 yard pink fabric 1 for Basket blocks background

1½ yards pale yellow fabric for alternate blocks

1 yard pink fabric 2 for inner border and binding

1⅛ yards pale green fabric for outer border

62″ × 62″ piece of batting

3½ yards backing fabric

Cutting

From the floral fabric:

Cut 4 strips 2⅞″ × the width of the fabric. Subcut into 41 squares 2⅞″ × 2⅞″. Cut these squares diagonally to make 81 half-square triangles (B unit).

Cut 1 strip 6⅞″ × the width of the fabric. Subcut into 5 squares 6⅞″ × 6⅞″. Cut these squares diagonally to make 9 half-square triangles (D unit).

From the pink fabric 1:

Cut 3 strips 2⅞″ × the width of the fabric. Subcut into 32 squares 2⅞″ × 2⅞″. Cut these squares diagonally to make 63 half-square triangles (A unit).

Cut 1 strip 6⅞″ × the width of the fabric. Subcut into 5 squares 6⅞″ × 6⅞″. Cut these squares diagonally to make 9 half-square triangles (C unit).

Cut 1 strip 4⅞″ × the width of the fabric. Subcut into 5 squares 4⅞″ × 4⅞″. Cut these squares diagonally to make 9 half-square triangles (F unit).

Cut 3 strips 2½″ × the width of the fabric. Subcut into 18 rectangles 2½″ × 6½″ (E unit).

From the pale yellow fabric:

Cut 2 strips 10½″ × the width of the fabric. Subcut into 4 squares 10½″ × 10½″.

Cut 2 squares 15½″ × 15½″. Cut these squares twice diagonally to make 8 quarter-square triangles for the side setting triangles.

Cut 2 squares 8″ × 8″. Cut these squares once diagonally to make 4 half-square triangles (these are the corner setting triangles).

From the pink inner border fabric 2:

Cut 5 strips 2½″ × the width of the fabric.

From the pale green outer border fabric:

Cut 6 strips 5½″ × the width of the fabric.

Piecing

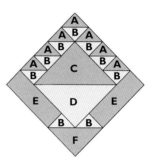

May Basket block

Directions below are for 1 basket. You will make a total of 9 baskets. Numbers on the diagrams indicate step numbers.

1. Piece 7 A units to 7 B units to make the basket handle squares.

2. Piece a row of 3 handle squares.

3. Piece a row of 4 handle squares.

4. Sew 2 B units to the 2 E units as shown, being careful to reverse 1 of the units.

5. Sew the C and D units together to create the center of the basket.

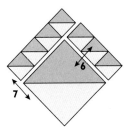

6. Attach the 3-square handle piece to the right side of the center basket piece.

7. Attach the 4-square handle piece to the left side of the center basket piece.

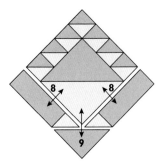

8. Attach the long rectangle units to the bottom of the basket.

9. Sew the final F unit to the bottom to complete the block.

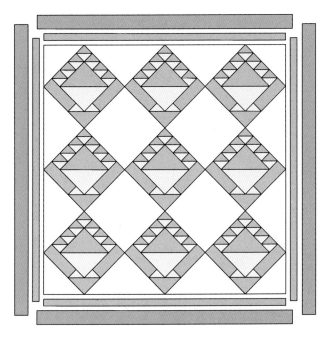

10. Arrange the Basket blocks, alternate blocks, and setting triangles according to the layout.

11. Assemble in diagonal rows first, then sew the rows together to create the center of the quilt. Use conventional methods to attach the inner and outer borders.

May Baskets layout

KENSINGTON COTTAGE 1, 2 & 3: 62˝ x 62˝
© 2006 Christine Maraccini

Pieced by Diane Woods, Antioch, CA

Quilted by Christine Maraccini

Fabric by Robert Kaufman Fabrics

Kensington Cottage

KENSINGTON
COTTAGE 1
"dragger"

KENSINGTON COTTAGE 1: *Edge-to-edge free-motion quilting*

This is the most versatile all-over design that I use. This technique is so popular that every machine quilter has his or her own version that he or she uses on a regular basis. I like to add free-form feathers in mine and mix in flower and leaf shapes when appropriate. This is the next step up once you've learned how to do the Heat Wave (page 20). Again, since this design has so many curves in it, it adds softness to a quilt that has many straight lines, such as this Double Irish Chain.

Edge-to-Edge Feather Medley ✧

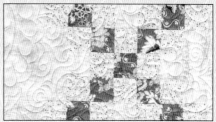

Feather Medley fill

Here are some additional shapes to add to the medley as you work:

1. Start the medley by creating a basic free-form feather. Begin this by making a vein. I prefer one with a slight wave to it.

2. When you reach the end, form the first bubble on the feather. These bubbles should be somewhat of an oval or teardrop shape and should not touch the vein.

3. Continue making these feathers down the vein, headed toward the beginning.

4. When you reach the start, sew right up to the point where you started and change directions, moving back up the vein.

5. Create the feathers in the opposite direction.

6. Once you reach the top, make the final feather pointing straight out from the top of the vein. At this point you should begin to echo and add in swirling, flowering, curving shapes. Try to maintain an even density as you move. If you get stuck in a corner, simply echo your way back out. Once you are a ways from the first feather, drop in another one. Try to get this one to go in a different direction from the first so that the design has an organic feel.

A. This is the shape that you learned in the Heat Wave pattern (page 20).

B. This is like the Heat Wave shape, but add a few scallops as you echo.

C. This is a basic spiral.

D. Add leaf shapes as you move around this basic spiral.

E. This is a spiral with scallops surrounding it—the basic Cabbage Rose shape (page 53).

F. A long curved spiral adds a nice break to dense quilting.

KENSINGTON COTTAGE 2
"keepsake"

KENSINGTON COTTAGE 2: *Free-motion quilting of increasing intricacy*

I love a traditional pieced quilt with slightly modern quilting. Instead of standard grid quilting, I chose a wiggling line. This is easier to free-motion quilt and will hide any uneven points your quilt might have. The large empty spaces in this quilt are a terrific canvas to show off a little free-motion design. Adjust that design a little and you have an easy free-motion border. Try this one out and your quilt will be done in no time.

Cabbage Leaf Square ■ ● ▲

I chose a Cabbage Leaf for this quilt because it matches the fabric. This formula also works for almost any leaf you know how to sew. Try it with the Spike Leaf and the basic leaf; you will love how it turns out. The squares on the edges of the quilt are not complete squares, so I adjusted the pattern to have only three leaves fitting into the portion of the square that is in the quilt.

Cabbage Leaf square

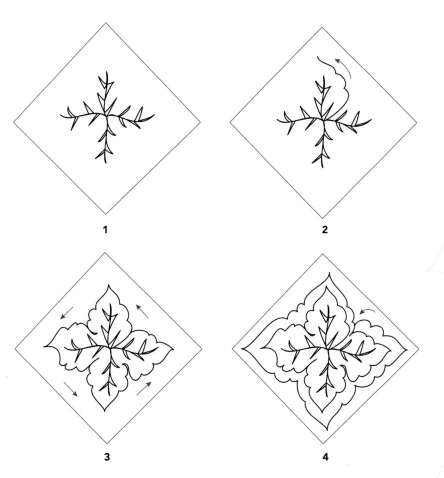

1   2

3   4

1. Starting in the center of the square, create veins that radiate toward each corner. Be sure to leave room at the ends for the leaf stitching. Start in the middle and end in the middle.

2. Curving out from the center, begin to make the first leaf around a vein. I generally add 2 or 3 curves and a pointed leaf tip.

3. Continuing around the center, begin the next leaf as you finish the first. Then complete the next 2 until you reach the first leaf, whose thread line you should touch.

4. Exit that spot and echo all the way around. Finish by stopping your stitching at the echo line for the first leaf.

Echo Lace Border S - M

So easy and so cute! Of course this one looks terrific on a feminine or baby quilt. This is best for use on a narrow or medium-width border. Once it gets over 3 inches, it starts to look a little odd.

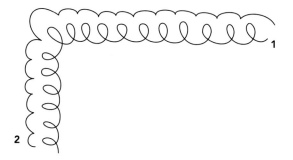

Echo Lace border

1. Start by doing a simple cursive e or row of loops all the way around the border. Finish sewing where you started so there is no visible start or stop.

2. Starting in a new spot, sew scallops that echo over each loop. Finish sewing where you started so there is no visible start or stop.

Echo Leaf Border M - L

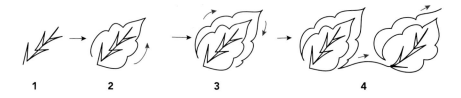

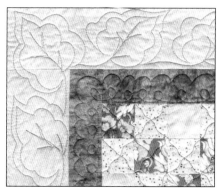

Echo Leaf border

1. Begin by sewing the vein in first. Do this by sewing a line at an angle, tracing back down a short way, then adding another vein. Come back to the center vein, sew down a little, then out and back to add another vein, and so forth, alternating the sides the veins point toward.

2. For this particular leaf, add 2 curves on the side of the leaf, then a basic leaf shape to the tip of the leaf and then another 2 curves to return near the base. Leave room around the leaf for the echo sewing. Don't touch the base of the leaf when you come back to the bottom.

3. Now echo your shape, returning to the base but not touching it.

4. Sew a slight curve and start the next leaf. Make sure you start the next leaf far enough from the first to have enough space for the echo sewing.

Try this formula with some of the other leaves that you learn in this book. This is a quick and easy way to match your border treatment to the quilting in the center of your quilt.

KENSINGTON
COTTAGE 3
"showstopper"

KENSINGTON COTTAGE 3: *Intricate free-motion quilting with trapunto*

A Double Irish Chain like this one has great space for trapunto. I designed this trapunto pattern to match the fabric in the quilt. It's a very classic design with a contemporary feel. The feathers on the outer border are a modern twist on the old favorite. This style of feather is easier to execute than a traditional round feather and is therefore easier to master. Refer to page 91 for the trapunto pattern for this quilt and to pages 84–87 for a step-by-step lesson on machine trapunto.

Cotton Blossom Fill

This is such a cute fill and has a pretty traditional feel. I've used it on Civil War prints and on pastel reproduction fabrics. For this quilt I chose to fill the chain path with this fill to de-emphasize the path so we can focus on the trapunto.

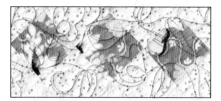

Cotton Blossom fill

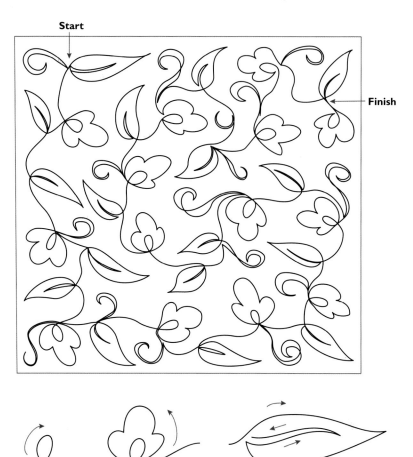

1. Form a teardrop or seed shape.

2. Echo over the teardrop with 3 scallops, forming a bonnet shape. Touch the base of the teardrop and head out to make the next shape.

3. The leaf for this one is a long flat leaf to match the one in the fabric. It's the same basic leaf that we have been using, just elongated a bit (refer to page 76).

Scrollwork Border   S-M

I love the look of wrought iron, and this border fits the bill. This is a great generic small-to-medium border.

Scrollwork border

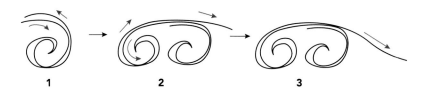

1. Leaving space for the left curl, sew forward to the right, making the right half of the scroll first. Curl down and then trace back on the same line to form one half of the scroll. Don't try to be perfect on the trace back; the space that's left open fills out the scroll.

2. As you stitch back to the top, stitch over your beginning lines to hide the starting point and curl to the left. Trace back to the top of the scroll.

3. Exit the scroll and sew toward the bottom side of the border to start the next scroll.

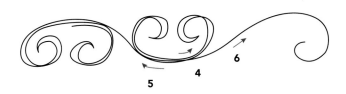

4. Leaving space for the left half of the scroll, make a curl to the right, then trace back.

5. Fill in the empty space by making the curl to the left then returning to the bottom of the scroll.

6. Exit the scroll and sew toward the other side of the border to start the next scroll.

Olive Leaf Feather Border M-L

This is my favorite feather. Of course I can do a traditional feather—it's just that I prefer the natural, organic feel of this one. It's so easy, but it looks so fancy.

Olive Leaf Feather border

1. The basic feather shape is more like a flower petal with a vein. Create the petal as illustrated.

2. Make the vein after putting the petal on.

3. Start the next petal touching the first.

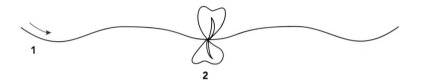

1. Begin the spine 1″ from the end of the border. Gently undulate the spine so that it has a nice flow. With a long border, draw the spine with chalk first so that the spacing is even.

2. At the center of the border, sew 1 petal straight up and 1 petal straight down. This is the point where the petals change the direction of their tilt.

3. As you reach the opposite end of the border, make the petals that run along the top side of the spine. Tilt the petals away from the center of the border.

4. When you come to the center petals you sewed in Step 2, be sure the last petal fits snugly against the center petal. Begin moving to the left, changing the tilt of the petals so that they point in the opposite direction of those on the right side.

5. When you reach the end, create 1 petal that points straight off the end of the spine. Camouflage your starting point by sewing a petal or vein over it. Continue along the underside of the spine just as you did the top side.

6. When you reach the end, make 1 final petal that sticks straight out from the end of the spine. If you are quilting this feather around all 4 sides of your quilt, be sure to mesh the corner petals together as shown in the quilt photo.

Kensington Cottage (Basic Double Irish Chain) Piecing

Quilt is 62″ × 62″

Blocks are 10″ × 10″

Inner border is 2″ wide

Outer border is 4″ wide

Fabric

1½ yards light fabric

¾ yard dark chain fabric

1¼ yards medium chain fabric

⅝ yard blue inner border fabric

1 yard pale pink outer border fabric

⅝ yard binding

67″ × 67″ piece of batting

3¾ yards backing fabric

Cutting

From the light fabric:

Cut 4 strips 2½″ × the width of the fabric.

Cut 2 strips 6½″ × the width of the fabric.

Cut 2 strips 10½″ × the width of the fabric. Subcut into 12 rectangles 6½″ × 10½″.

From the dark fabric:

Cut 9 strips 2½″ × the width of the fabric.

From the medium fabric:

Cut 16 strips 2½″ × the width of the fabric.

From the blue inner border fabric:

Cut 6 strips 2½″ × the width of the fabric.

From the pale pink outer border fabric:

Cut 6 strips 4½″ × the width of the fabric.

Piecing

1. Make 2 strip sets A using 1 light, 2 medium, and 2 dark 2½″-wide strips for each set. Cut the strip sets into 26 segments 2½″ wide.

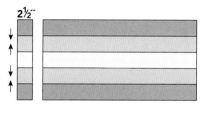

Strip set A; make 2.

2. Make 2 strip sets B using 3 medium and 2 dark 2½″-wide strips for each set. Cut the strip sets into 26 segments 2½″ wide.

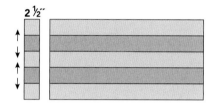

Strip set B; make 2.

3. Make 1 strip set C using 2 light, 2 medium, and 1 dark 2½″-wide strips. Cut the strip set into 13 segments 2½″ wide.

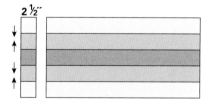

Strip set C; make 1.

4. Make 2 strip sets D using 1 light 6½″-wide and 2 medium 2½″-wide strips for each set. Cut the strip sets into 24 segments 2½″ wide.

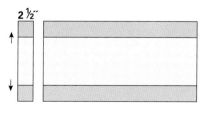

Strip set D; make 2.

5. Assemble 13 Chain blocks using 2 A segments, 2 B segments, and 1 C segment for each block.

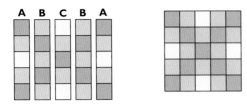

6. Assemble 12 alternate blocks using 2 D segments and a light 10½″ × 6½″ rectangle for each block.

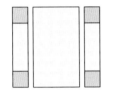

7. Arrange the Chain and alternate blocks according to the layout diagram. Sew the blocks together in rows. Then sew the rows together to create the center of the quilt. Use conventional methods to attach the inner and outer borders.

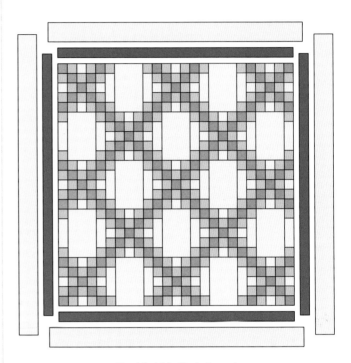

Double Irish Chain layout

Savvy Stars

SAVVY STARS 1, 2 & 3: 44" x 44"

© 2006 Christine Maraccini

Pieced by Cheryl Uribe, Livermore, CA

Quilted by Christine Maraccini

Fabric by Michael Miller Fabrics, LLC

SAVVY STARS 1
"dragger"

SAVVY STARS 1: *Edge-to-edge free-motion quilting*

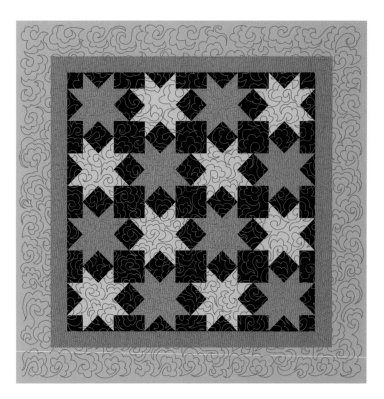

This is a similar concept to the Heat Wave pattern. Just add some curls and scallops and you have a nice floral pattern. The texture and feel of this quilting make for a very cozy quilt. Since it is such a curvy design, it complements a quilt with many straight lines and sharp points, such as this Sawtooth Star pattern.

Edge-to-Edge Cabbage Rose Echo ✧ ▦

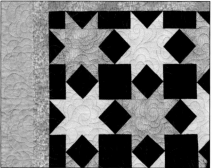

Cabbage Rose Echo fill

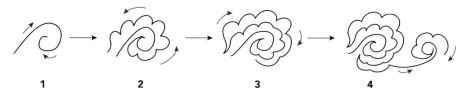

1   2   3   4

1. Create the first curl in the direction you plan to head toward.

2. Sew small scallops back toward your beginning point. Be careful not to touch the beginning curl line; we need the negative space to pop through there.

3. Echo back over the first set of scallops. A good rule of thumb is to use the width of the quilting foot to space the echo.

4. Exit the rose and start the next curl to create the center of the next flower. Be sure to constantly change directions so you don't end up with a long row of roses. Keep in mind that the direction of the hook is the direction you will be landing in when the rose is complete.

SAVVY STARS 2
"keepsake"

SAVVY STARS 2: *Free-motion quilting of increasing intricacy*

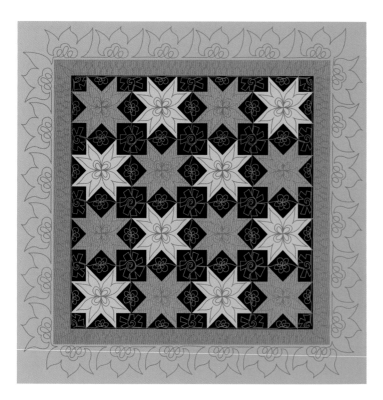

There is an often-ignored path created by Sawtooth Stars when they are placed next to one another. It's a chain of square–square-on-point–square and so on. For this quilt I alternated a Chicory Flower and a Double Daisy across each path. Once done, I turned the quilt and sewed the missing Double Daisies in the perpendicular path. My connector lines ran through and around the existing Chicory Flowers. At the sides, I made half a flower to fill the half-square left by the piecing.

Passion Flower

Finding a shape that fits into a Sawtooth Star can be pretty difficult. Many people give up and just stitch in the ditch or do close echo quilting inside the star. This flower gives you an option that is both fanciful and quick.

Passion Flower

1. Sew a teardrop or seed shape toward the right-hand quadrant of the Sawtooth Star.

2. Echo back, keeping a relatively close distance (approximately $1/8''$) to the first line of stitching.

3. Create a long leaf shape that reaches into the first spike of the star.

4. Come back toward the seed shape but don't touch it. Head toward the second spike of the star, creating the second leaf shape.

5. Repeat this process for the next quadrant, then the third and fourth.

6. Finish the flower back where you started, hiding your stopping stitches on top of your starting stitches.

Chicory Flower

This is such a cute flower; I couldn't resist showcasing it in the black path left by the Sawtooth Stars. Do these flowers in a row one after another or add a few leaves to make a funky border for a kid's quilt.

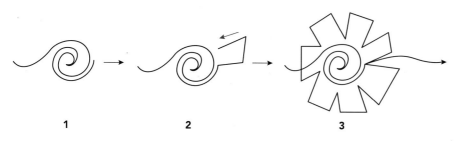

1   **2**   **3**

Chicory Flower

1. Start your Chicory Flower by creating a tight swirl and echoing back to the center side of the swirl.

2. At this point begin making squared petals. Don't let your stitches touch the center swirl as you come back in.

3. Continue making the petals until you come back to where you started the first petal. Let your stitching touch the stitches of the first petal so the flower will be closed. You are now in position to head toward the next flower or element.

Double Daisy

The daisy is such a versatile element. It can be just a simple daisy or it can be the center of a more intricate flower. First learn the quick way to sew a five-petal daisy and then add any combination of outer petals to make a fancy flower. For this one, I opted to echo the daisy center to make a sweet little flower to alternate with the squared Chicory Flower.

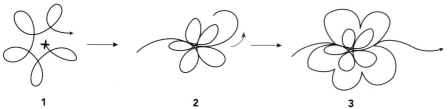

1   **2**   **3**

Double Daisy

1. This illustration is spaced out to show the direction for stitching a simple 5-petal daisy. Begin at the X and make a continuous looping motion passing through the center of the flower. While practicing you will notice that there is a rhythm to it. Once you have this committed to your muscle memory, it will be easy.

2. This is what the daisy looks like when you make the loops closer together. If you sewed each petal separately and didn't loop through the center there would be a larger buildup of thread on the petals since you do a lot of backtracking.

3. Echo the daisy petals to create the Double Daisy.

Up/Down Loop Border S-M

This border is a good generic small-to-medium border. It's a good one to use to separate too many floral quilting designs, as in this quilt.

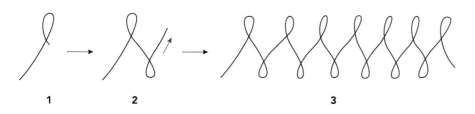

Up/Down Loop border

1. Begin with a diagonal line, creating a teardrop-shaped loop at the top. Leave at an angle headed down.

2. Make the next teardrop loop as you approach the bottom of the border.

3. Try to keep the spacing as even as possible and maintain a regular slant while moving from each loop to the next as you move around the quilt.

Artichoke Border M-L

It's not really an artichoke, but that's what I think of when I see the outer spikes on this border. This one is quite a chameleon. It will blend nicely on a floral or vegetable quilt, or it can just be a snazzy addition to a geometric quilt like this one. For this particular quilt, the Artichokes are approximately 6˝ in width.

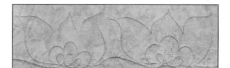

Artichoke border

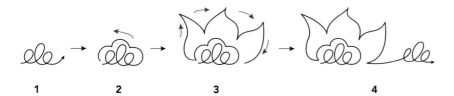

1. Start by making 3 loops, one after another. I like to make the center one slightly larger.

2. Echo back over these loops, creating 3 loose scallops.

3. Without touching the stitching where you started, sew 3 fat leaf shapes over the scallops.

4. Complete the last leaf shape without touching the scallops and head back out to start the next motif.

SAVVY STARS 3
"showstopper"

SAVVY STARS 3: *Intricate free-motion quilting with trapunto*

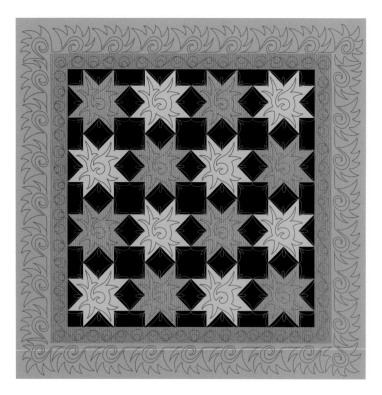

This is such a fun and cheery quilt. I wanted to demonstrate that trapunto can be done on colored fabrics. Add in a little variegated thread and these simple Sawtooth Stars come to life. Refer to page 92 for the trapunto pattern for this quilt and to pages 84–87 for a step-by-step lesson on machine trapunto.

Curves & Teardrops ■ ▲

I'm not a big fan of stitching in the ditch. I also don't like to do a lot of starts and stops. This quilting design will allow you to quilt across the entire quilt and back before you need to stop. That's what I call efficient!

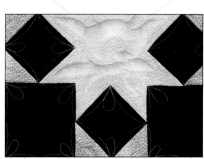

Curves & Teardrops

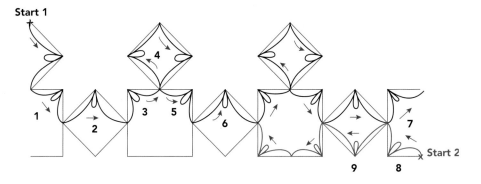

1. Start at one corner and make a soft curve until you reach the next corner. At that point sew a teardrop shape extending slightly into the square. Next make a soft curve until you reach the next corner.

2. Sew into the next 2 squares as illustrated.

3. Sew into the next square, completing one corner. This puts you in place to enter the square-on-point above.

4. Moving clockwise, complete the entire square-on-point as illustrated.

5. Return to the bottom square and quilt toward the right.

6. Again, sew 2 sides of the square-on-point and continue as you did in Steps 3–5.

7. When you reach the end you will need to stop and tie off.

8. Start again (at Start 2), heading toward the left.

9. You will be quilting only the bottom half of the squares and will not be extending into the squares-on-point that hang below.

10. As you reach the far left side, continue sewing down the left side of the quilt to put yourself in position to repeat this path toward the right as illustrated.

Double Bubble Border   S

This is another one of those very versatile borders. Use it on a floral quilt and it will look like seeds. Use it on a kid's quilt to add some whimsy. This border pattern will flatten out the entire border and leaves little negative space. That is great when you need a simple transition from one area to another.

Double Bubble border

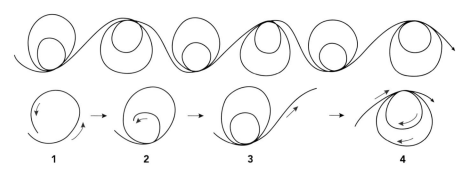

1. Start by making the outside circle. When you start with the inner circle the bubbles tend to be too big.

2. Come back around and cross over to make the inner circle when you reach the edge of the outer circle. This is extremely important if you want to keep your bubbles lined up.

3. Start the next bubble, continuing with the same looping motion you used for the first circle. Cross over at the same point you crossed over the first circle, right next to the seamline.

4. Change directions and begin the next circle as you reach the opposite seamline. Again, create the outer circle and then continue on to make the center. Once this unit is complete, change directions and start the next circle on the opposite side of the border.

Porcupine Border   M - L

I like how this border echoes the spiked look of the Sawtooth Stars. It is great on celestial quilts and quilts that have a lot of curves.

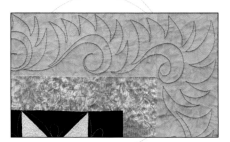
Porcupine border

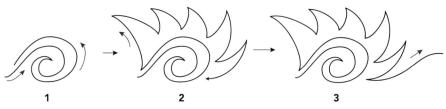

1. Start by making a tight curl to the right and echoing back.

2. Begin making spikes that lean to the left. Do not touch the curl as you sew toward the center; you want to leave the negative space open.

3. Echo back as many times as necessary to reach the rightmost end of the curl. There is no rule about how many spikes you must use; it will depend on the width of your motif. Exit the motif and sew to the right to start the next curl.

SAVVY STARS PIECING
(BASIC SAWTOOTH STAR)

Quilt is 44″ × 44″

Blocks are 8″ × 8″

Inner border is 2″ wide

Outer border is 4″ wide

Fabric

$\frac{1}{2}$ yard green fabric for stars

$\frac{1}{2}$ yard pink fabric for stars

$1\frac{1}{2}$ yards black fabric for background and binding

$\frac{3}{8}$ yard orange fabric for inner border

$\frac{7}{8}$ yard green fabric for outer border

49″ × 49″ piece of batting

$2\frac{3}{4}$ yard backing fabric

Cutting

From the green fabric:

Cut 3 strips $2\frac{7}{8}$″ × the width of the fabric. Subcut into 32 squares $2\frac{7}{8}$″ × $2\frac{7}{8}$″. Cut these squares diagonally to make 64 half-square triangles (A unit).

Cut 1 strip $4\frac{1}{2}$″ × the width of the fabric. Subcut into 8 squares $4\frac{1}{2}$″ × $4\frac{1}{2}$″ (D unit).

From the pink fabric:

Cut 3 strips $2\frac{7}{8}$″ × the width of the fabric. Subcut into 32 squares $2\frac{7}{8}$″ × $2\frac{7}{8}$″. Cut these squares diagonally to make 64 half-square triangles (A unit).

Cut 1 strip $4\frac{1}{2}$″ × the width of the fabric. Subcut into 8 squares $4\frac{1}{2}$″ × $4\frac{1}{2}$″ (D unit).

From the black background fabric:

Cut 3 strips $5\frac{1}{4}$″ × the width of the fabric. Subcut into 16 squares $5\frac{1}{4}$″ × $5\frac{1}{4}$″. Cut these squares twice diagonally to make 64 quarter-square triangles (B unit).

Cut 4 strips $2\frac{1}{2}$″ × the width of the fabric. Subcut into 64 squares $2\frac{1}{2}$″ × $2\frac{1}{2}$″ (C unit).

From the orange inner border fabric:

Cut 4 strips $2\frac{1}{2}$″ × the width of the fabric.

From the green outer border fabric:

Cut 5 strips $4\frac{1}{2}$″ × the width of the fabric.

Piecing

1. Piece 32 pink and 32 green star point units as shown.

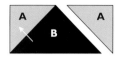

Make 32 pink and 32 green units.

2. Piece 8 pink and 8 green Sawtooth Star blocks, according to the diagram, and press.

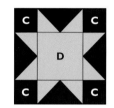

Make 8 pink and 8 green blocks.

3. Arrange the pink and green stars according to the layout. Piece together in rows first, then sew the rows together to create the center of the quilt. Use conventional methods to attach the inner and outer borders.

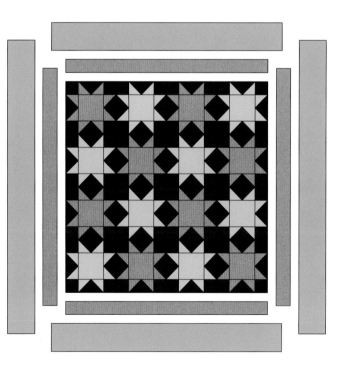

Sawtooth Stars layout

Solar Twist

SOLAR TWIST 1, 2 & 3: 55″ X 55″
© 2006 Christine Maraccini

Pieced and quilted by Christine Maraccini

Fabric by RJR Fabrics

SOLAR TWIST 1 "dragger"

SOLAR TWIST 1: *Edge-to-edge free-motion quilting*

This edge-to-edge design is one of the quickest ways to get a quilt finished. It will add visual movement to the Pinwheel design and has a texture and feel that beg the owner to cuddle up in it. On domestic machines the tendency is to make these curls very small. Resist that tendency and go for a nice large curl, about 2 to 3 inches across. You want to feel the softness of the fabric and batting when you touch this quilt, not the stiff buildup of thread that results from quilting lines that are too close together.

Blustery Day fill

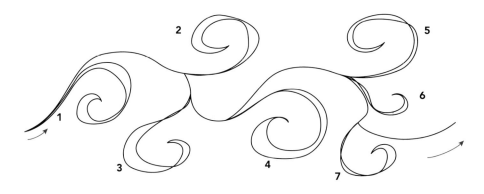

Make your first curl and trace back. Don't worry about tracing exactly on the same line; a little space between stitch lines adds to the 3-dimensional quality of the curl. Sew back to the base of the curl and then head back out, changing directions to start the next curl. Change directions between each curl to produce a softly undulating design.

Follow my numbers to see which order I sewed the curls in. This should be a random process, changing directions and sizes often. If you attempt to make all the curls the exact same size, you will likely fail and it will be apparent. So, go ahead and make the sizes vary. It will look more natural.

SOLAR TWIST 2: *Free-motion quilting of increasing intricacy*

SOLAR TWIST 2
"keepsake"

The Pinwheel quilt has started to appear everywhere. Various books teach how to cut a repeated pattern from fabric to achieve a kaleidoscope affect when the pieces are sewn together in a Pinwheel shape. Although the Pinwheel is the feature element, be sure not to ignore the interesting negative space created when the Pinwheels are pieced side by side.

Curls for 8-Blade Pinwheel 🌼 ●

This is a simple treatment for a Pinwheel; however, you need to follow my directions for piecing the block and remember to press your seams open. You might not want to quilt heavily in the center of the block if there is a large lump of fabric formed by the overlapping seams. This design works great on a circle—just sketch in a few lines to break the circle into even spaces to stitch the curls.

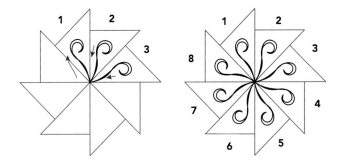

8-Blade Pinwheel

1–8. The illustration is pretty clear on this one. Start the first curl at the center of the Pinwheel and continue clockwise until each blade has a curl (refer to the diagram for Edge-to-Edge Blustery Day on page 64 to make the curls).

Palm Frond Square ■ ● ▲

This motif works great in this background space but it's also a good option for a square area.

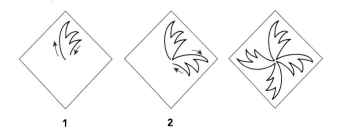

Palm Frond square

1. Start sewing at the center of the background square. The piecing will give you a very clear center point. Quilting up, sew the first Palm Frond into the negative space (refer to Step 1 in the diagram for the Palm Frond border page 67).

2. Moving in a clockwise direction, sew each Palm Frond until you come back to the center, hiding your last stitches.

Undulating Curl Border S-M

So easy—this is a terrific generic border for a small-to-medium path.

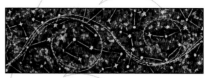

Undulating Curl border

1. Sew the first curl and trace back over the line. Don't worry about being exactly on the line; a little bit of space adds to the 3-dimensional look of the design.

2. Sew back to the base of the curl and then head back out, changing directions to start the next curl.

3. Change directions between each curl to produce a softly undulating design.

Palm Frond Border L

This border was designed to complement the quilting in the background spaces. The motifs are approximately 4″ wide in this particular quilt.

Palm Frond border

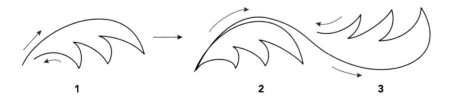

1. Starting near the bottom edge, curve gently up, make a point, and then make 3 spikes as you move back toward the base of the frond.

2. Trace over the back of the frond and change directions to start the next frond.

3. Repeat the steps to continue around the border.

SOLAR TWIST 3
"showstopper"

SOLAR TWIST 3: *There is no trapunto on this quilt*

This quilt has celestial fabrics so I quilted it with theme-appropriate designs. Again, note that the Candle Flame design fits neatly into the background spaces but would work just as well in a square. Notice that there is a lack of trapunto in this quilt. With the number of seams and the dark fabric, I knew that trapunto would be wasted effort. It simply would not have shown up.

Spinning Sun

I used a metallic thread for this design to add sparkle to the Pinwheel. Again, it will look like a flower on a floral quilt. Try it in a circle shape or adjust the design to have a different center (i.e., daisy or other small flower).

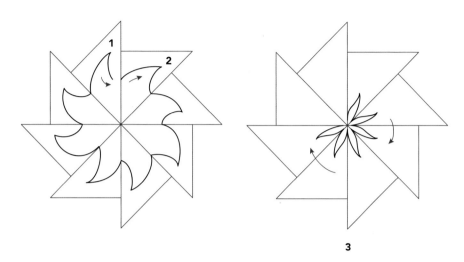

Spinning Sun

3

4

1. Start sewing about ⅓ of the way down one of the Pinwheel seams. Curve out and hook back in, somewhat like the blade of a circular saw.

2. Continue around the Pinwheel in the same way, and when you make the last blade, stop at the same spot where you began the first blade.

3. For the center quilting, start at the natural center of the Pinwheel and make long, skinny leaf shapes. Move in a clockwise direction, being sure to give each Pinwheel blade a leaf. Stop sewing in the same spot as where you started.

4. Depending on the fabric in your quilt, this will either be interpreted as a sun or as a flower.

Candle Flame Square ■ ● ▲

I love this shape. On a floral quilt it will appear to be a flower. This motif will fit in a square as well as in this background space.

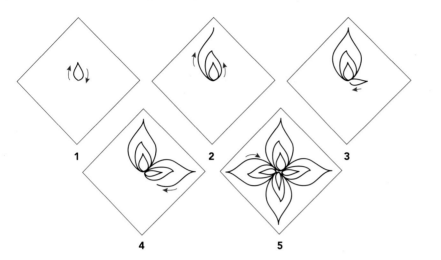

Candle Flame square

1. The piecing of the Pinwheel quilt creates an obvious center to the background spaces. Start sewing at the center and create a fat flame shape, moving in a clockwise direction.

2. Echo over it once, then a second time. This will leave you in position to start the next flame.

3. Again sewing in a clockwise direction, make a small flame shape and repeat Step 2.

4. Moving around in a clockwise direction, place each echoed flame into the negative space left by the Pinwheels.

5. As you finish the last flame, hide your ending stitches in the same spot as your starting stitches.

Twisted Rope Border   S

This is a great alternative to a traditional rope border that requires a lot of starting and stopping.

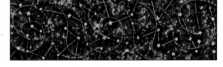

Twisted Rope border

1. Start with a flame shape tilting to the left. As you exit the flame, make a single curl toward the flame.

2. Echo back over the curl, leaving space for the fabric to show through. Slope down and to the left as you approach the edge of the border.

3. Make another flame shape that tilts toward the open curl and curves around it.

4. Continue this pattern around the border. When approaching a corner, space the motif so that the flame shape lands in the corner of the border, pointing diagonally away from the center of the quilt.

Flame Border L

This is a single-sided feather with an echo. It's my absolute favorite. Looks great with metallic thread!

Flame border

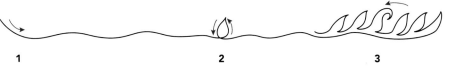

1. Start at one end and softly undulate the vein approximately ⅛″ to ¼″ above the seamline.

2. When you reach the centermost spot of the border, make 1 flame pointing straight up.

3. Continue down the border until you get close to the end. Start sewing back toward the center with the flames tilting away from the center. Add in a few swirls or wave shapes.

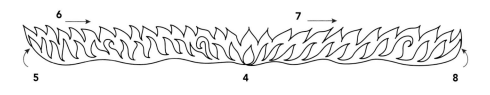

4. When you get to the center flame, sew under it and continue on the other side, changing the direction of the tilt so the flames will lean away from the center.

5. When you make the last flame, be sure to sew over your starting point so that it will blend in and disappear.

6. Sew up and begin making echo flames over the top of the first set of flames. Again, tilt them away from the center, but sew toward it.

7. When you reach the center flame, sew the echo flame straight up and then change directions, tilting the flames away from the center again.

8. When you reach the end, finish sewing by attaching your stitch line to the first flame below the echo.

SOLAR TWIST
(BASIC PINWHEEL) PIECING

Quilt is 55″ × 55″

Blocks are 10″ × 10″

Inner border is 2½″ wide

Outer border is 5″ wide

Fabric

¾ yard light gold fabric for Pinwheels

¾ yard dark gold fabric for Pinwheels

1⅓ yards blue fabric for background

½ yard red/brown fabric for inner border

1⅛ yards yellow fabric for outer border

½ yard blue fabric for binding

60″ × 60″ piece of batting

3⅜ yards backing fabric

Cutting

From the light gold Pinwheel fabric:
Cut 3 strips 6¼″ × the width of the fabric. Subcut into 16 squares 6¼″ × 6¼″. Cut these squares twice diagonally to make 64 quarter-square triangles.

From the dark gold Pinwheel fabric:
Cut 4 strips 4⅜″ × the width of the fabric. Subcut into 32 squares 4⅜″ × 4⅜″. Cut these squares diagonally to make 64 half-square triangles.

From the blue background fabric:
Cut 3 strips 6¼″ × the width of the fabric. Subcut into 16 squares 6¼″ × 6¼″. Cut these squares twice diagonally to make 64 quarter-square triangles.

Cut 11 strips 2″ × the width of the fabric. Subcut into 64 rectangles 2″ × 6″.

From the red/brown inner border fabric:
Cut 5 strips 3″ × the width of the fabric.

From the yellow outer border fabric:
Cut 6 strips 5½″ × the width of the fabric.

Piecing

1. Sew each of the dark gold half-square triangles to the blue background rectangles as shown to make 64 A units. Trim the excess background fabric as shown. Press toward background fabric.

Trim —

Make 64 A units.

2. Sew each of the light gold quarter-square triangles to the blue background quarter-square triangles as shown to make 64 B units. Press toward the background fabric. Then sew each A unit to a B unit as shown to make 32 C units. Press toward B.

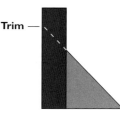

B

A

3. Piece together 2 C units to make half a Pinwheel block. Press the seam open between the 2 units. This will eliminate bulk at the center when the halves are sewn together.

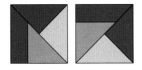

4. Once all the halves are made, line them up and sew each pair of halves together to produce the completed Pinwheel blocks. Again, press the seam between the 2 halves open to reduce bulk in the center of the Pinwheel. It is much easier to quilt the blocks when you press these seams open.

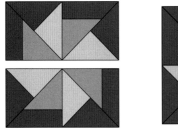

5. Arrange the Pinwheel blocks according to the layout diagram. Sew the blocks together in rows. Then sew the rows together to create the center of the quilt. Use conventional methods to attach the inner and outer borders.

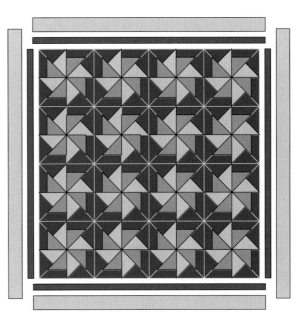

Pinwheel layout

Butterfly Garden

BUTTERFLY GARDEN 1, 2 & 3: 57″ X 57″
© 2006 Christine Maraccini

Pieced by Christie Batterman, San Ramon, CA

Quilted by Christine Maraccini

Fabric by Robert Kaufman Fabrics

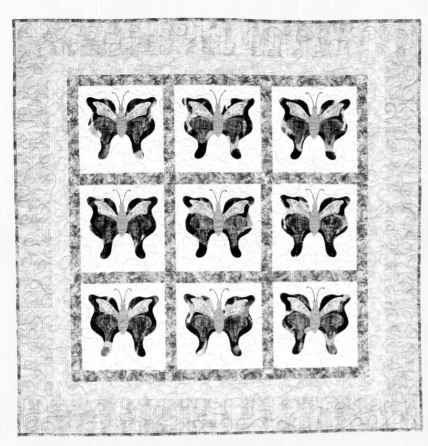

BUTTERFLY
GARDEN 1
"dragger"

BUTTERFLY GARDEN 1: *Edge-to-edge free-motion quilting*

It's a little challenging to quilt an edge-to-edge design on an appliqué quilt. To determine the spacing of the flowers, lay your basted quilt out on a flat surface. Begin to place pins sparsely over the quilt in a somewhat random order to indicate flower placement. Make sure that none are too close together or too far apart. As you quilt, when you come to one of these pins you will know that you need to place a flower there. Fill in the rest of the space with curls and leaves. Be sure to quilt near the appliqué, but not over it. For this design, I quilted a $\frac{1}{4}$″-offset echo around the inside of the wings of the butterflies to keep the quilting simple. Refer to page 93 for the appliqué pattern for this quilt.

Edge-to-Edge Balloon Flower ✧

This is a versatile edge-to-edge design that I use a lot. Change the flower and the leaf to match the fabrics of your quilt and it is custom quilting every time.

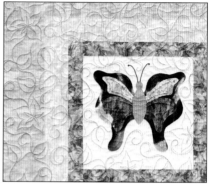

Balloon Flower fill

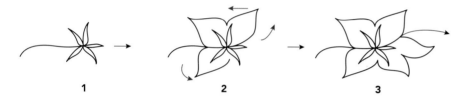

1. Start a Balloon Flower by making a star-shaped center. This is done by making 5 small, skinny leaf shapes radiating from the center (think: head-arm-leg-leg-arm as you sew).

2. Starting in the direction you plan to head, exit the center star and start making leaf-shaped petals centered over each star point. Move around the flower until it has all 5 of its petals.

3. Let the stitching of the last petal touch the first petal to close the flower. Stitch out from that point to start the next element.

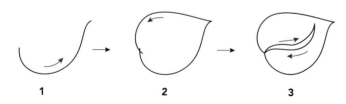

1. Begin a basic leaf by creating the bottom curve.

2. Sew back to meet the base.

3. Add a vein, sewing back to the base and out.

4. Refer to Steps 1 and 2 of the Undulating Curl Border on page 67 to add curls.

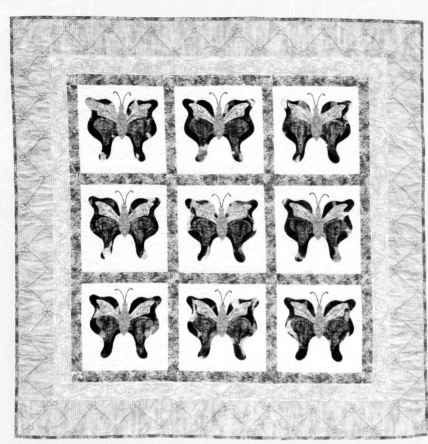

BUTTERFLY GARDEN 2: *Free-motion quilting of increasing intricacy*

BUTTERFLY GARDEN 2
"keepsake"

This quilt should be called *Crazy for Daisies*. I use them so much that I wanted to share their versatility with you. Substitute any small or medium flower for the daisies in these designs and you will have brand-new ideas for your quilts. Note the simple meander with the daisies in the white around the butterflies. This is a nice way to fill around an appliqué element without having to fall back on the basic meander. I've also done a simple set of curls in each butterfly wing to tack down that area without piling on too much thread.

Simple Daisy Border   S-M

Daisy after daisy after daisy. Simple and sweet, this design will only work on a small-to-medium border. Refer to page 56 for the steps to make a basic Daisy.

Simple Daisy border

Curl Leaf Border   M

Pretty and modern. Practice this one to get the rhythm down.

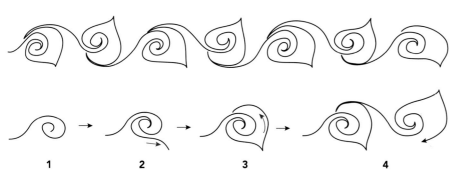

Curl Leaf border

1. Sew a tight curl in the center of the border.

2. Echo back out and begin to make a leaf shape pointing toward the seamline.

3. Make the other side of the leaf shape, connecting with the top of the curl.

4. Change directions and make the next curl in the opposite direction of the first.

Daisy Lattice Border   M-L

This border works well on garden-theme quilts or those that have plenty of curves. Try substituting another flower to match your fabric. Measure your border and map this one out to make it fit correctly.

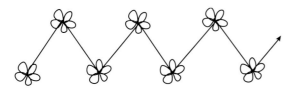

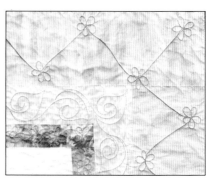

Daisy Lattice border

For this quilt, the daisies are 3 inches apart. Use pins or a water-soluble blue pen to give yourself a target for each daisy (see Double Daisy, page 56).

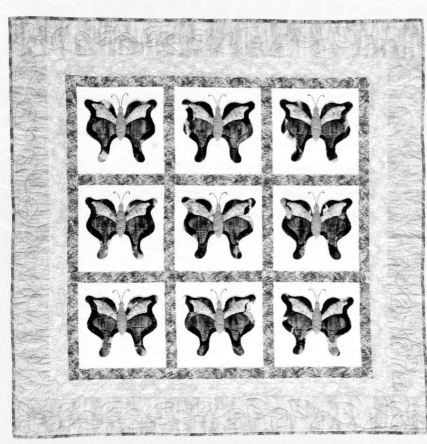

BUTTERFLY GARDEN 3: *Intricate free-motion quilting with trapunto*

BUTTERFLY GARDEN 3
"showstopper"

Appliqué provides you with a natural pattern for trapunto. There is no need to mark your quilt! Although you could add detail stitching inside the trapunto, avoid depressing too much of the area. Most of the time I opt to stitch in the ditch around the pieces of the trapuntoed appliqué, like I did for these butterflies.

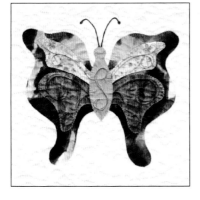

Basic Leaf Border   S - M - L

Keep in mind that these leaves are running in a certain direction. Mark your map and your quilt so that you always know which direction the leaves should head in each border. It's easy to forget once the quilt is rolled up and ready to sew on.

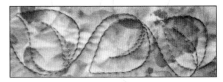

Basic Leaf border

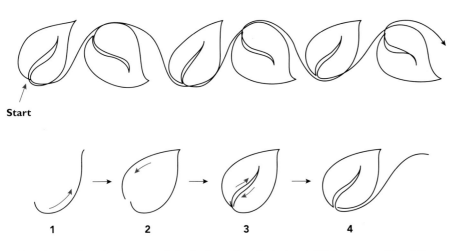

Start

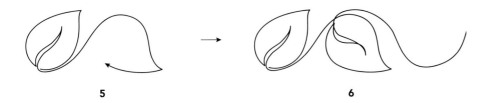

1   2   3   4

1. Start by making the bottom of the leaf, angling it at about 45° from one side of the border to the other.

2. Be sure to make a sharp point on the leaf, then curve back down to the base of the leaf.

3. Place a nice curvy vein in the leaf, extending about ¾ the length of the leaf.

4. Leave the leaf and curve toward the opposite edge of the border to start the next unit. Notice that all connector lines are **between** the leaves.

5   6

5. Each time you start a leaf you are starting with the outermost edge and finishing with the inner side.

6. Be sure to change directions with every leaf to maintain a graceful flow.

Cornerstone Quilting ■

Because this quilt has cornerstones between all the sashes, I like to put a daisy in those spots. This enables me to hide my connector lines at these very busy junctions. With these types of inner sashes I start by sewing in all the horizontal borders (Direction A); then I turn the quilt and sew in the vertical sashes (Direction B). When completing the vertical sashes you will meet up with the daisy that you put in previously. Simply stitch from the last leaf through the center of the daisy and start the leaf in the next sash. This is a cool trick to keep starts and stops to a minimum.

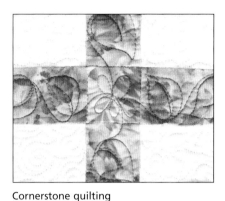

Cornerstone quilting

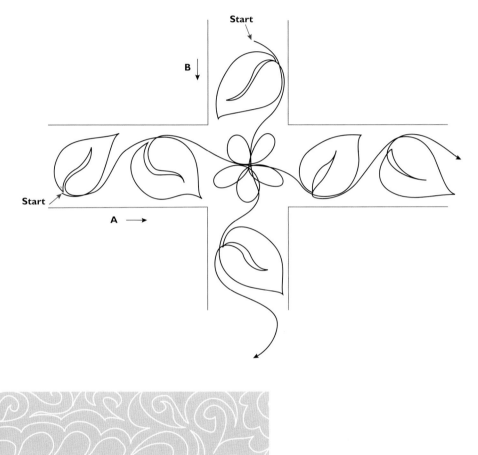

Leaf Tendril Lattice Border S - M - L

It looks tricky, but it just takes some practice. There is a rhythm to this border, so draw it many times before you quilt it. Measure your border and mark with pins or blue pen dots so that your motifs are evenly spaced. The ones in this quilt are approximately 1½ inches apart.

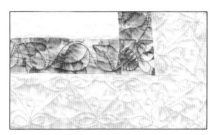

Leaf Tendril Lattice border

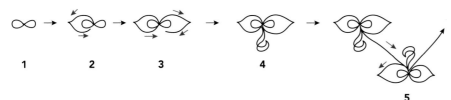

1   2   3   4   5

1. Begin with an elongated figure-8 shape.

2. Echo over one side with a fat leaf shape.

3. Cross over at the center and sew a leaf over the second half.

4. Once you reach the center, sew a tiny curl and then sew back facing in the direction that you want to stitch.

5. Angle down to the other side of the border and make another Leaf Tendril.

Balloon Leaf Border & Corner Treatment   L

For this border design I used a variegated thread and started by placing a Balloon Flower (instructions on page 76) in the corner. From there I sewed a Basic Leaf border. Because this border is so big, the leaves are quite large and needed a three-pronged vein in the center to keep the density relatively consistent. This vine of leaves extended to the center of the quilt. Once finished, I started at the flower and made a vein trailing down the side of the quilt and stopping at the center. This was done on all four corners of the quilt. The top left and bottom right borders are in a variegated thread and the opposite corners are in a thread that matches the fabric.

Balloon Leaf border & corner treatment

BUTTERFLY GARDEN (BASIC APPLIQUÉ) PIECING

Quilt is 57″ × 57″

Blocks are 12″ × 12″

Sashing is 1½″ wide

Inner border is 2½″ wide

Outer border is 5″ wide

Fabric

1⅝ yards white fabric for appliqué blocks

1¾ yards total various fabrics (lavenders, grays, pinks) for butterfly appliqué

⅝ yard purple fabric for sashing

¼ yard light green fabric for cornerstones

⅝ yard yellow fabric for inner border

1⅛ yards lavender fabric for outer border

½ yard green fabric for binding

62″ × 62″ piece of batting

3½ yards backing fabric

Cutting

From the white fabric:
Cut 3 strips 13½″ × the width of the fabric. Subcut into 9 squares 13½″ × 13½″. (After appliquéing the butterflies on the background, you will trim the blocks down to an accurate 12½″ × 12½″.)

From the purple sashing fabric:
Cut 8 strips 2″ × the width of the fabric. Subcut into 24 rectangles 2″ × 12½″.

From the light green cornerstone fabric:
Cut 1 strip 2″ × the width of the fabric. Subcut into 16 squares 2″ × 2″.

From the yellow inner border fabric:
Cut 5 strips 3″ × the width of the fabric.

From the lavender outer border fabric:
Cut 6 strips 5½″ × the width of the fabric.

Piecing

1. Copy the Butterfly appliqué pattern on page 93. Flip the pattern to complete the body and make a template. Trace the wing and the wing details to make separate templates for each.

2. Use any appliqué method you like to prepare and cut the fabrics. You will need 9 each of all the wing parts and 9 of the wing parts reversed. You will need 9 bodies.

3. Center a butterfly on a 13½″ × 13½″ background square. Attach the large wing piece first, then layer the wing detail pieces and finish with the body on top. Place the appliquéd block on top of the pattern and draw in the antennae with a water-soluble pen. Stitch the antennae with a satin stitch on your sewing machine or embroider by hand. Repeat to create the other 8 appliqué blocks.

4. Trim the appliquéd blocks to 12½″ × 12½″.

5. Sew 12 sashing strips and 16 cornerstones into 4 vertical rows according to the diagram below.

6. Sew sashing strips to the bottoms of all of the appliqué blocks. Also add sashing strips to the tops of 3 of the blocks. Sew these into 3 vertical rows.

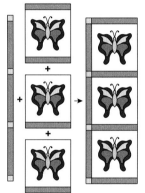

7. Attach the 3 rows of appliqué blocks to 3 sashing/cornerstone vertical rows as shown.

8. Sew the vertical appliqué block/sashing rows together and add the fourth sashing/cornerstone row to make the center of the quilt. Use conventional methods to attach the inner and outer borders.

Trapunto – The Easy Way

WHAT IS TRAPUNTO?

Trapunto is a form of quilting in which the design is outlined with two or more rows of stitching and then padded from the underside to achieve a raised effect. The trapunto masterpieces of our ancestors were hand quilted, and the extra batting would have been stuffed into little slits in the back of the quilt, causing a particular motif or design to puff up higher than the rest of the quilt. These quilts were most often pure white and had no piecing (also known as wholecloth). Although this classic style of hand quilting produces beautiful results, the same can be accomplished with a sewing machine.

Machine-quilted trapunto has traditionally been looked down upon as inferior to the hand-quilted kind, but times are changing. By no means should you fool yourself into believing that machine trapunto is a quick process. Although it is more time efficient than hand quilting, it takes the same amount of preparation and planning prior to the sewing, and executing a good trapunto fill is an acquired skill. With a moderate amount of practice, you too will be including trapunto in the design of your favorite quilts.

Supplies & Tools

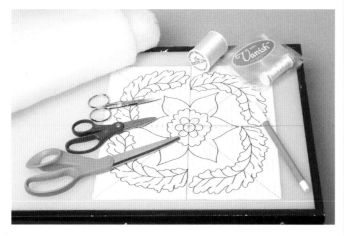

Trapunto requires special tools that are easy to use once you understand them.

  Blue water-soluble pen

  Water-erase pen

  A variety of scissors

  Stencil or photocopied pattern

  Light box

Trapunto Batting

When choosing a trapunto batting, look for a brand that is dense and thick. I like to use high-quality polyester batting with a loft of 16 to 20 ounces. Since I have a stockpile of it, I have also been known to use a double layer of Hobbs Polydown. Watch out for the inexpensive battings that have a high loft but little density. These will compress in your quilt and you will lose the trapunto effect.

Water-Soluble Thread

I prefer Vanish Extra by Superior Threads. Because water-soluble thread is delicate, be sure to lower the top tension in your sewing machine to prevent breakage. When finished, be sure to store your dissolvable thread in a sealed bag to keep out moisture.

Extra-Fine Polyester Thread

Choose thread to match your fabric. I prefer Highlights or The Bottom Line by Superior Threads. These threads are very fine but maintain their strength. The importance of a fine thread is that it will virtually disappear on your quilt, hiding any mistakes that you may make during the quilting.

Quilt Wash

Available at most quilt shops, this is soap made to be gentle on your quilt.

Water-Soluble Pen

When using a water-soluble pen, follow these basic rules:

1. Always wash your fabrics prior to marking on them since sizing and stabilizing chemicals in the fabric can react with the ink.

2. Once the fabric is marked, do not allow the ink to get hot or it may set the chemical into the fabric (ironing and leaving your quilt in a hot car are both heat hazards).

3. Using water only makes the blue ink disappear temporarily. After the quilt is finished you must wash your quilt with a quilt-safe soap to completely remove the chemical from the fabric and batting.

TRANSFERRING THE PATTERN TO THE QUILT TOP

The first step in this method is to mark your quilt top. If you are using a pattern from a book or magazine, make a copy of it and place the copy on a light box. Position the quilt top over the pattern and trace the design onto the fabric with a water-soluble pen. I prefer to use photocopied patterns because I can resize them on a copy machine to fit my quilt top. If you are using a prepared stencil, simply place it on top of the quilt and draw inside the grooves with a water-soluble pen. Use a water-erase pen to correct any mistakes. If the quilt has appliqué designs, there is no need to mark it before sewing in the trapunto batting.

ATTACHING THE TRAPUNTO BATTING

The second step in the process is to sew the trapunto batting onto the back of the quilt top. If you are using a longarm machine, use batting the same size as the quilt top. Pin up the batting as though it were the backing and lay the quilt on top of it. If you are using a domestic machine, use batting the same size as the quilt top or pieces slightly larger than each individual trapunto design. Pin baste the batting to the back of the quilt top. Load a water-soluble thread in the top of your machine and fill the bobbin with a fine polyester thread in a color that matches the quilt fabric. Free-motion quilt around the outermost lines of your design. There is no need at this point to quilt the detail lines inside the trapunto. Depending on the pattern you chose, you may also need to quilt inside the trapunto design to create a center hole. For instance, if you are using a feathered wreath pattern, you will need to remove the batting from around the outside of the wreath as well as from the center of the wreath. Only the feathers themselves need extra batting under them.

The purple thread represents the stitching that would be done with dissolvable thread to hold the trapunto batting onto the back of your quilt top.

TRIMMING EXCESS BATTING

The next step is my favorite, because it's something I can do while sitting at my kids' sports practices. You need to trim away all the excess batting from the edge of the trapunto design. Test a few different kinds of scissors for this. I like a large pair of blunt-nose scissors for getting the bulk of the batting cut away. Then I use a sharp, pointy pair of embroidery scissors for the close trimming. Experiment to figure out what works best for you; there is no strict rule here.

Trim away the excess batting from every area that you don't want to stand out.

In the event that you accidentally snip into your quilt top, don't panic. I assure you: it happens to everyone. Mark the area with your blue water-soluble pen so that you will find it later in the process. When it comes time to quilt, you will layer and baste the three components of the quilt. If there is a small flap of the snipped fabric still attached to the quilt top, put a small dab of water-soluble basting glue on the back of it and glue it in place. If there is no fabric left and you have a hole, make a small patch from extra fabric and glue that to the inside of the hole. When sewing, be sure to go over this area with extra density and your problem will completely disappear.

THE ART OF TRAPUNTO QUILTING

Now you have a marked quilt top with trapunto batting sewn into the areas where the trapunto will be located. Layer and baste the quilt as usual but add a few extra pins or basting stitches in and around the trapunto areas for extra stabilization. Put the water-soluble thread away and put fine polyester thread on the top of your machine and thread the needle. Whew! It's finally time to quilt.

There are a variety of ways to quilt the dense stitching around the trapunto. A traditional method is to sew straight lines extremely close together in a crosshatch formation, diagonal, straight, or radiating from the center of the square. Although beautiful, this method requires a lot of starting and stopping. I prefer to utilize free-motion designs that I can complete without having to stop until the area is finished. Choose from the dense fill designs below or make up one of your own. Start by sewing around and into the detail lines of the trapunto and filling around it as you go.

These are a variety of fills that work wonderfully to depress the area around your trapunto. From left to right are Micro-stipple, Spiral Medley, and Leaf Echo Micro-fill.

Micro-stipple

This is the garden-variety basic stipple. Keep your stitches curved and change directions often. This fill looks somewhat like a bunch of puzzle pieces or a meandering line. Don't worry if your stipple doesn't look exactly like mine; the key is to have the stitching lines *very* close together.

Spiral Medley

This fill is very similar to the Feather Medley that was presented on page 41—just leave out the feathers. I like this one because it allows me to quilt very close to irregularly shaped trapunto. Throw in swirls, teardrops, and spikes, but keep all the stitching close together.

Leaf Echo Micro-fill

This is just like the Heat Wave quilting that was presented on page 20. Instead of starting with a teardrop shape, start with a leaf shape that has no vein. This fill is terrific when you are quilting around a floral trapunto because it sticks to the theme.

Keep the fill around the trapunto very dense. Because you are using a fine thread it is easier to keep your design compact while hiding most of your mistakes. Quilt the rest of the top as usual.

THE CRITICAL STEP: WASHING & BLOCKING

There is a strange phenomenon occurring throughout the quilting realm. For some reason, quilters have an aversion to washing their quilts. It is a necessary step in finishing and preserving your masterpiece. When doing trapunto it is *crucial* that you wash and block your quilt; however, it is something you should do with *every* quilt you complete.

1. Start by filling your washing machine with warm water (cold water will not dissolve the water-soluble thread as well as warm) and a quality quilt wash. Once the basin is full, submerse your quilt in the water, hand agitate, and allow it to soak for 15 minutes. Do not allow the washing machine to agitate your quilt; it's best to do it by hand.

2. Run the spin cycle to remove the water and let the basin fill up again with clean water to rinse the quilt. Again, hand agitate. Run the spin cycle once again to remove the bulk of the water from the quilt.

3. Lay the quilt on a carpet in your home or lay towels down and place it on the towels. Do not hang your quilt to dry; it will distort from the weight of the water pulling on the fabric.

4. Get out your rulers and be sure that the corners are square and that each side of the quilt measures *exactly* the same. Pin the quilt to the floor so that it maintains its squared-up shape as it dries. *Cotton fabric has a good memory, and the shape that the quilt dries in is the shape that it will try to return to for the rest of its life.* In a household climate, your quilt should be completely dry in 8–12 hours.

Trapunto Patterns

Tahoe Retreat trapunto pattern C

Tahoe Retreat trapunto pattern A

Tahoe Retreat trapunto pattern B

May Baskets trapunto pattern A

May Baskets trapunto pattern C

May Baskets trapunto pattern B

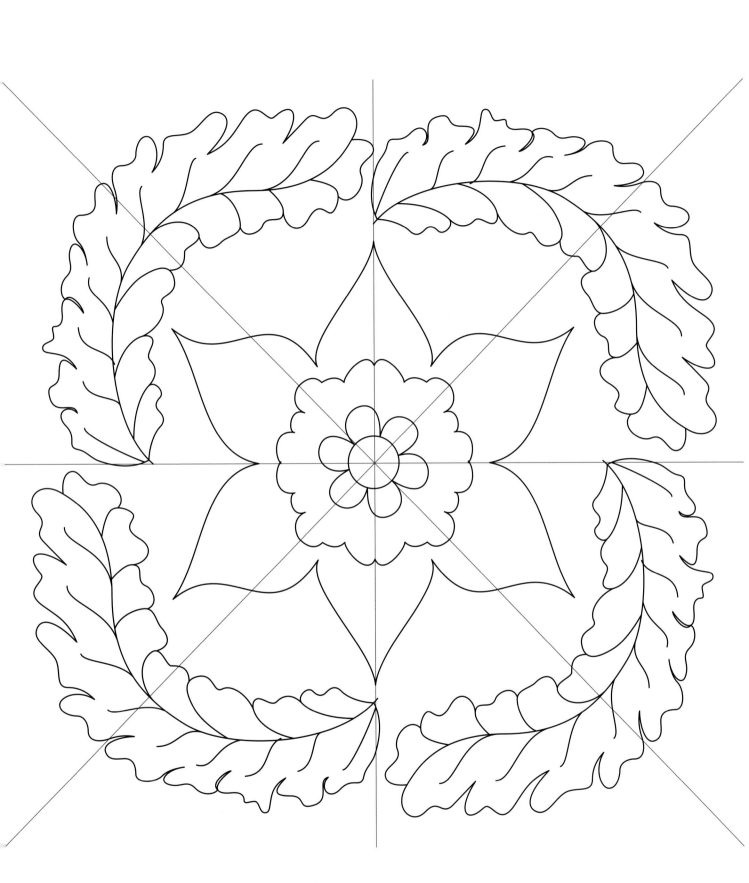

Kensington Cottage trapunto pattern

Savvy Stars trapunto pattern

Machine Quilting Solutions

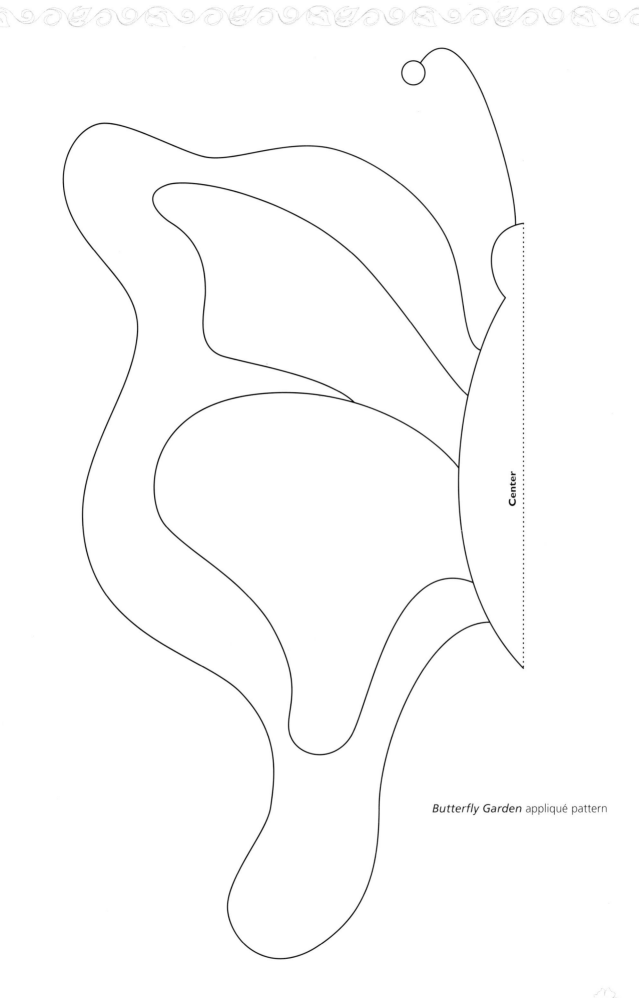

Center

Butterfly Garden appliqué pattern

Resources

C&T Publishing
Phone: (800) 284-1114
Website: www.ctpub.com
fast2fuse™ Interfacing
Double-Sided Fusible Stiff Interfacing
Quilter's Vinyl

The Cotton Patch
Mail order: 3405 Hall Lane, Dept. CTB
Lafayette, CA 94549
Phone: (800) 835-4418
Website: www.quiltusa.com

Michael Miller Fabrics, LLC
118 West 22nd St., 5th Fl.
New York, NY 10011
Phone: (212) 704-0774
Website: www.michaelmillerfabrics.com

RJR Fabrics
2203 Dominguez St., Bldg. K-3
Torrance, CA 90501
Phone: (800) 422-5426
Website: www.rjrfabrics.com

Robert Kaufman Fabrics
129 West 132nd St.
Los Angeles, CA 90061
Phone: (800) 877-2066
Website: www.robertkaufman.com

Superior Threads
PO Box 1672
St. George, UT 84771
Phone: (800) 499-1777
Website: www.superiorthreads.com

Timeless Treasures Fabrics, Inc.
483 Broadway
New York, NY 10013
Phone: (212) 226-1400
Website: www.ttfabrics.com

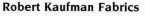

About
the Author

Photo by Rocky Moreno

Christine Maraccini discovered her love for
quilting many years ago when she decided to
put her sewing skills to work making baby
quilts for friends who were starting their families. She has been in love with this art
form ever since and continually looks for new approaches to the old standards.
Christine began a successful machine-quilting business in 2000 in order to stay
home to raise her young children. Since then she has received various awards on the
local and state level, had her work published in *American Patchwork and Quilting*, and
appeared on and helped create a quilt for ABC's *Extreme Makeover: Home Edition*.

Christine lives in the beautiful Gold Country of Northern California with her husband,
three children, and all of the critters that they bring home. She teaches fun and
intensive machine-quilting classes. Contact her at **www.christinescustomquilts.com**
to see where she will be next or to arrange for her to come to your area.